Corporate Contributions, 1990

by Anne Klepper

Contents

About the Author

Anne Klepper is a senior research associate in the corporate practices program. Previously, she headed the Board's contributions research and meetings program. Prior to joining The Conference Board, she was the President's Special Assistant and speechwriter, and later the Director of Corporate Contributions at Time Inc. Her publications include five *Annual Surveys, The Corporate Contributions Professional,* and *Corporate Social Programs: Nontraditional Assistance.* She inaugurated the series of *Outlooks* in the contributions field, the most recent being *Corporate Contributions in an Era of Restructuring.*

Acknowledgments

The author would like to thank Maria Buenaventura, Research Administrative Assistant, for her work in dealing with the mass of statistical data needed to produce this report. Analytical programming was provided by William Dole. Charts were prepared by Chuck N. Tow, Chief Chartist.

From the President

The Conference Board's Survey of Corporate Contributions, now in its 25th edition, provides executives with a detailed, comprehensive overview of corporate contributions based on information provided by 338 firms. This survey, sponsored by the Board and the Council for Aid to Education, enables executives to assess their programs against those of firms in the same industry, income or asset groups, or against firms headquartered in their region of the country, and to evaluate national trends.

The charts in the report clearly present important highlights, including trends in cash and noncash contributions, corporate assistance, and corporate beneficiaries.

The Conference Board appreciates the participation of the contributions executives who supply data for this survey every year. Their sustained support is essential to the quality of the information we are able to report.

PRESTON TOWNLEY
President and CEO

Introduction

Corporate contributions exploded dramatically in the '70s and '80s from $797 million in 1970 to an estimated $6 billion in 1990. For more than half those years, growth has occurred at double-digit rates. Even more remarkable, contributions grew when income before taxes dipped four times, in the periods 1975, 1980-1982, 1985-1986, and 1989-1990.

Such growth is unlikely in the foreseeable future. Unpredictability is the key fact about the corporate climate of the '90s. Mergers and acquisitions and leveraged buyouts may have slowed, but restructuring and reorganization continue apace—and downsizing is the name of the game. Less people, more demands. And the vise is tightened because of the crunch at all levels of government—federal, state and local.

Corporate contributions hovered near 1 percent of pretax income from 1961-1980. In the '80s, contributions rose from that mark to 2.34 percent in 1986. That peak percentage was partly due to the fact that some 1987 gifts were reported in 1986 to take advantage of the more favorable tax provisions (before effectuation of the Tax Reform Act of 1986). It was also partly due to the fall in corporate income. However, ever since 1982, contributions have exceeded the 1 percent norm of the '60s and '70s—and have been hovering at 1.7 percent to 1.9 percent for most of those years (see Table 1).

What of the future? There is commitment to communities where companies have headquarters, plants, facilities. Community involvement has always been, and will continue to be, a basic rationale for corporate contributions.

Contributions will continue to be made across the spectrum of the social agenda—health and human services, education, culture and the arts, civic and community activities. The emphasis will vary company by company. Education will remain the number one priority, and higher education will still take the lion's share of the corporate education dollar. It's obviously in business' interest to focus on the three R's—recruitment, research and development, retraining. It's that educated work force we count on to be competitive.

Precollege public education has come into the spotlight in recent years. While there has been an increase in charitable dollars, it has not been explosive. Many of the dollars are business expense from other areas of the corporation, particularly human resources. Much of the involvement is through personal activity—tutoring, mentoring, etc.

Business/education partnerships are too numerous to count. Some say there are some 100,000 business/education partnerships of a business and a school, with probably another 100,000 involving cities, government entities and civic organizations—a growth industry.

If the economy improves, so will contributions. Mild growth may be in the cards. If the economy does not grow, for contributions, as for other areas, it becomes a guessing game.

Contributions

This survey deals primarily with corporate charitable contributions. Since 1936, corporations have been allowed a deduction on their tax returns for charitable gifts. Charitable contributions include cash, product, and other property (land, buildings, securities, equipment other than the company's own product), and are 100 percent deductible. The Internal Revenue Code and regulations govern the evaluation to be used for product and other property.

Table 1 shows all Corporate Contributions and Corporate Income before and after taxes from 1936-1990. This is the only table in the report which shows total contributions of all corporations paying U.S. taxes. The other tables in this report are based on the data supplied by the 338 respondents to the 1990 survey. Contributions of survey respondents have generally constituted about one-third of total corporate giving.

In Table 1, IRS figures (1936-1988) are based on direct corporate contributions and corporate gifts *to* their company foundations. Council for Aid to Education estimates (1989 and 1990) reflect direct corporate contributions and gifts *by* company foundations. Most of the other tables show respondents' direct corporate giving and gifts by their foundations. This money flowing out to the beneficiaries is the essence of corporate contributions.

Carryforwards and Returns for Noncalendar Fiscal Years

Council for Aid to Education (CFAE) estimates for 1989 and 1990 also include carryforwards and returns for companies with noncalendar fiscal years. Since 1981, corporations can deduct up to 10 percent of taxable income for contributions. Contributions in excess of this amount may be carried forward and used as deductions for up to five years after the tax year itself.

Corporations may also claim as deductions contributions actually made in the first two and one-half months following the end of their fiscal year. As a result, the tax file in any given year includes returns for companies with fiscal years that end in the months through June of the following year, and some contributions may be made as late as September 15.

CFAE estimates that the $6 billion figure for 1990 may include about $400 million of gifts made by company foundations and $500 million of carryforwards and returns for noncalendar fiscal years.

Corporate Assistance

Survey data since 1982 have also included tables showing business expense corporate dollars flowing to six categories. These categories were developed in a special study on 1981 data which tracked a limited number of "social" expenditures other than charitable dollars. Some 50 possible categories were reduced to the six considered most important.

Pretax Income

In general, pretax income is income before federal, state and local income taxes. Property taxes, gross receipts taxes, and payroll taxes should be considered expenses and deducted from income.

Corporations can deduct up to 10 percent of "taxable income" as contributions since 1981 (from 1936-1981, it was 5 percent). Taxable income is a closely held, confidential figure which is not available. Pretax income is higher than taxable income.

Executive Summary

Contributions as a Median Percent of:

	1990	1989	1988
Worldwide Pretax Income:	1.0	0.9	0.8
U.S. Pretax Income:	1.2	*NA*	0.9

Where They Gave:

Share of Contributions Dollar Received*

	1990	1989
Education	38.5%	38.4%
Health and Human Services	28.3	26.4
Civic and Community	12.4	13.9
Culture and Arts	11.9	11.1
Other	7.2	7.6
Unspecified	1.8	2.4

* Figures do not add to 100 percent due to rounding.

The Largest Givers: U.S. Industries (330 Firms)

Ranked by Size of Contributions

Transportation equipment (17)	$222,514,000
Petroleum and gas (22)	$218,866,000
Pharmaceuticals (13)	$199,491,000
Computers/office equipment (9)	$196,535,000
Telecommunications (13)	$162,380,000
Chemicals (21)	$162,379,000
Retail/wholesale (14)	$128,930,000
Insurance (35)	$123,789,000

The 1991 Outlook

Of the 338 companies responding to the survey, 259 provided estimates of their 1991 budgets. The direction? Slower growth than predicted for 1990. Overall, the 1991 anticipated median percentage increase was 1.6 percent, down from the 2.7 percent projected for 1990 (see Table 24). Service companies expected a 3 percent increase for 1991, down from 4 percent for 1990 (see Table 23). Manufacturing companies saw a sluggish 0.29 percent increase for 1991 versus 1 percent for 1990.

As was the case last year, companies with the smallest budgets predicted the largest increases. Companies with budgets under $1 million anticipated increases of about 4.5 percent. Companies with budgets of $5 million and over forecast increases of only 0.9 percent—60 percent of what they had estimated last year for 1990 (1.5 percent).

How Much They Gave

A core group of 233 companies (referred to as "matched cases") participated in 1989 and 1990. These are larger donors, contributing a median amount of $2,863,884. The median percent change from 1989-1990 for this group was 5 percent—less than the 8.8 percent change in 1988-1989 (see Table 4).

What They Gave

Cash	88%
Product	9
Property and Equipment	3

The move toward more cash giving continues (see Table 11). In 1989, cash giving was 85 percent; in 1988, cash peaked at 89 percent. From 1984-1987, cash accounted for 78 percent of the total.

Product, at 9 percent, is a shade under the 10 percent given in 1989. Product was in the 10-12 percent range from 1984-1987. Three industries report particularly heavy product donations in 1990: pharmaceuticals (number one again), 31 percent; computer/office equipment, 29 percent; and print/publishing/media, 17 percent. Food/beverage/tobacco records a drop to only 6 percent in 1990, less than half its 1989 level.

Property and equipment gifts are 3 percent of the total (down from 5 percent in 1989). However, the property percentage is subject to wide fluctuations since one very large gift can substantially alter the proportion (as was the case in 1987 when there was a single gift of $90 million and the property percentage was 10.4 percent). Before 1987, property was around the 9-10 percent mark.

Where They Gave: The Beneficiaries

Data reveal no surprises here. "Stability" is the key characteristic in the apportioning of the contributions dollar. Education is number one again at 38.5 percent (see Table 3). This dominant trend is likely to continue for the rest of the decade. The percentage has been around the 37-38 percent mark for many years (the 42.9 percent shown in 1986 was aberrant since it included a very large one-time property gift).

Higher education takes the largest share at 20 percent (up from the 1987-1989 share). Precollege education accounts for 2.8 percent (about the same as in the last two years). As noted in the introduction, many of the dollars in this area are business expense (particularly in human resources), and much of the effort is through nonmeasurable individual involvement.

Health and human services receives 28.3 percent. This figure is up from the 26.4 percent in 1989, but remains in line with the percentages since 1983. (It should be noted that in any given category fluctuations of 1-2 percentage points are not meaningful.) Federated giving is up a shade—12.8 percent versus the 11.9 percent of the previous year.

Culture and arts at 11.9 percent is right where it has essentially been for the last decade. No decline yet in this category, despite much rhetoric. What 1992 will bring is as yet unknown.

Civic and community is down a shade at 12.4 percent versus 13.9 percent in 1989. It has been in the 12-14 percent range in the past five years, with no major fluctuations.

A definitional note about "Other" and "Unspecified": "Other" covers gifts to U.S. groups whose primary objective is aid in other countries (such as CARE) and charitable support for special sports and patriotic events (such as the Olympics). "Unspecified" was added to the beneficiary breakouts in 1988 to cover those dollars not clearly allocated to specific categories.

Foundation Payouts and Payins

A major trend: Foundations are paying out more than is coming in at a faster rate. In the past six years (with the exception of 1986), company foundations gave away more dollars than they got from their corporations (see Tables 20, 21, 22). In 1989, company foundations gave away *nearly twice* what they took in. In 1990, company foundations gave away *more than twice* what they received ($889.2 million versus $414.6 million).

There is an ill wind blowing in the company foundation world. Some companies are drawing down their foundations. Others are waiting for more profitable times before they give their foundations more monies. The economy and the tax laws will be the major determinants of foundations' futures. So far, no silver linings have appeared.

Overseas Giving

In 1990, 87 companies report making contributions outside the United States. Fifty-one companies supplying data on dollars spent a total of $137,021,723. This is up substantially (17 percent) from the $117.5 million reported by 63 companies in 1989. The 1990 median donation of $429,000 is also up dramatically (52 percent) over the 1989 median of $282,800. These increases *may be* signals of increased activity on the global scene by the major international players. But the numbers should be viewed with caution since the inclusion (or exclusion) of a few major players can dramatically alter both totals and medians.

In 1988 and 1989, the total amount of overseas giving was virtually the same. As a result, 1990 is a real jump. The median for overseas contributions has been rising for three years, from $174,000 in 1988 to $429,000 in 1990—a giant 147 percent increase. This is especially interesting since the number of companies reporting overseas dollars has not shown a comparable increase.

Contributions per Employee

The median gift per employee is at a new high— $217.22. There has been a steady climb in contributions per employee since 1984 (with the exception of 1987).

1984	$125
1985	137.5
1986	162.5
1987	156
1988	175
1989	191
1990	217.22

Median giving per U.S. employee for 1990 is up for all groups except in companies with 2,500-4,999 employees (where it is flat) and in companies with 25,000-49,999 employees (where there is a drop from $210-$174). The percentage increase is the largest in the smallest companies. In companies with less than 1,000 employees, the median is up 46 percent; in companies with 1,000-2,499, the median is up 28 percent. It should be noted that reduced staff will boost the amount per employee if the budget stays the same.

Administrative Costs

When analyzed by size of contributions budget, median administrative costs in 1990 range from 4.2 percent (for the largest budgets of $5 million and over) to 6.9 percent (see Table 18). This spread is much smaller than in 1989, when costs ranged from 4.3 percent to 9.4 percent (for budgets from $500,000 to $1 million). This decrease would seem to indicate that companies are getting a handle on a relatively uniform percentage cost for contributions budgets, irrespective of size.

On the other hand, the median cost of running the contributions function rose to $162,000, up from $142,500 in 1989. Median costs in 1988 ($83,500) and 1987 ($99,900) dropped from $135,100 in 1986.

The high dollar median cost in 1990 is not a good omen. Administrative dollar costs are likely to be pared in this era of belt-tightening.

Survey Administration

The questionnaire used to collect 1990 data was longer than the 1989 form and differed from it in several respects. Information was requested on U.S. sales, assets, pretax income and number of employees (as it had been in 1988 and earlier years). More detail was asked for in the four major categories: health and human services, education, culture and the arts, and civic and community. A special section requested information on contributions to organizations outside the United States. Two special sections sought extensive information on precollege education.

The questionnaire was mailed in March 1991 to the Fortune 1000, to all previous cooperators, and to 100 foreign firms with major subsidiaries in the United States. In June 1991, a special short form was mailed to 529 companies that had not yet responded to the long questionnaire. The questionnaire was addressed to a named contributions manager whenever possible. There was some follow-up with companies who provided 1989 data but who failed to report 1990 data.

There were 338 usable questionnaires returned—a response rate of 23 percent. In 1989, 333 questionnaires were usable. The aggregate contributions reported by 1990 survey participants ($2.07 billion) amount to 35 percent of estimated total contributions by all U.S. corporations (see Table 1).

Charts

Contributions and Income Before Taxes, Current and Constant Dollars, 1973 to 1990

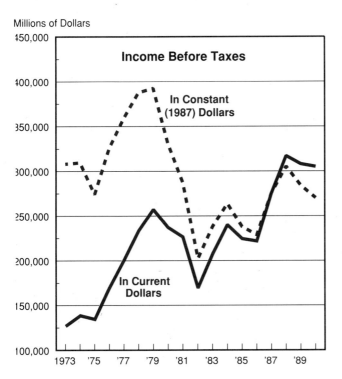

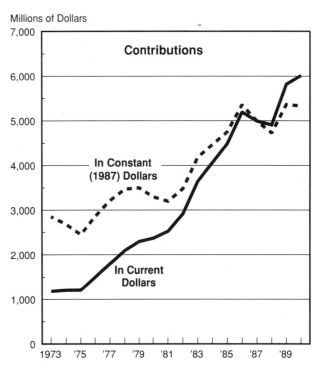

Chart 2:

Percentage Change in all Corporate Contributions and Income Before Taxes in Constant Dollars, 1973 to 1990

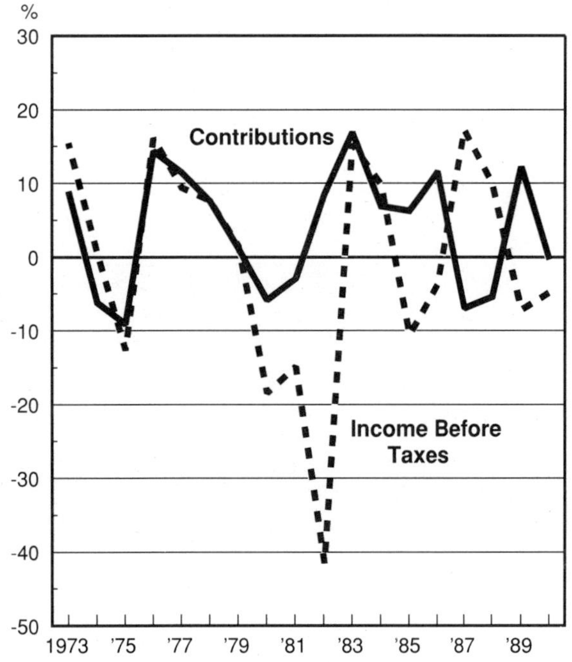

%

30

20

10

0

-10

-20

-30

-40

-50

1973 '75 '77 '79 '81 '83 '85 '87 '89

Contributions

Income Before Taxes

Note: 1989 and 1990 are based on estimates

Chart 3:

Distribution of Contributions Dollar

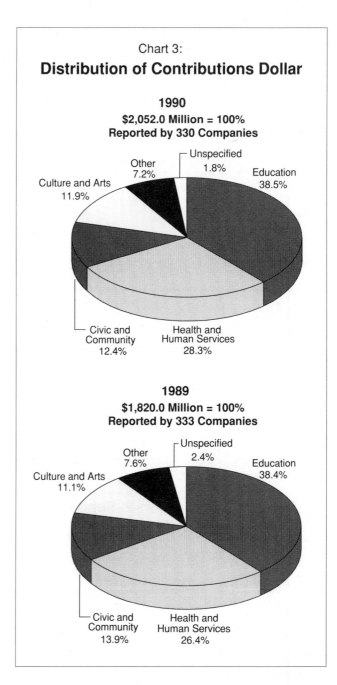

1990
$2,052.0 Million = 100%
Reported by 330 Companies

Other 7.2%

Unspecified 1.8%

Culture and Arts 11.9%

Education 38.5%

Civic and Community 12.4%

Health and Human Services 28.3%

1989
$1,820.0 Million = 100%
Reported by 333 Companies

Other 7.6%

Unspecified 2.4%

Culture and Arts 11.1%

Education 38.4%

Civic and Community 13.9%

Health and Human Services 26.4%

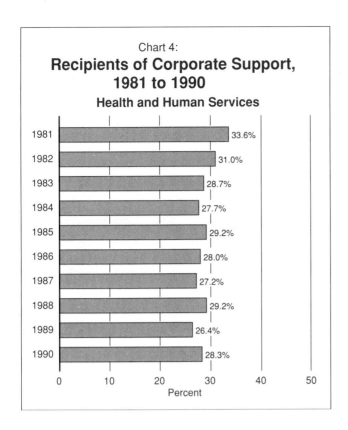

Chart 4:
**Recipients of Corporate Support,
1981 to 1990**
Health and Human Services

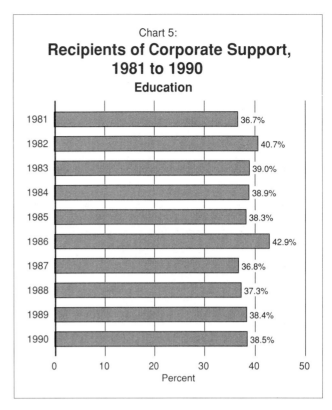

Chart 5:
**Recipients of Corporate Support,
1981 to 1990**
Education

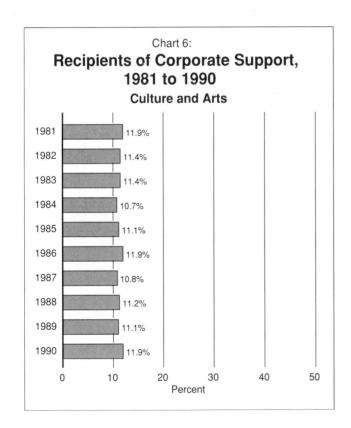

Chart 6:
**Recipients of Corporate Support,
1981 to 1990**
Culture and Arts

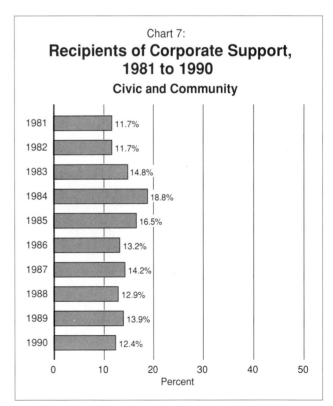

Chart 7:
**Recipients of Corporate Support,
1981 to 1990**
Civic and Community

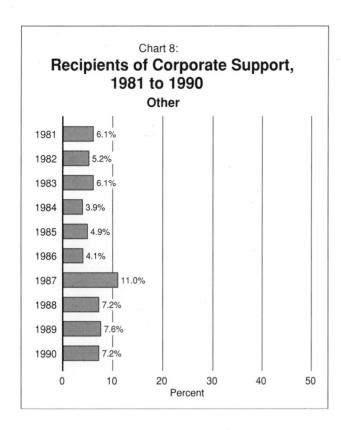

Chart 8:
**Recipients of Corporate Support,
1981 to 1990**
Other

Year	Percent
1981	6.1%
1982	5.2%
1983	6.1%
1984	3.9%
1985	4.9%
1986	4.1%
1987	11.0%
1988	7.2%
1989	7.6%
1990	7.2%

Percent

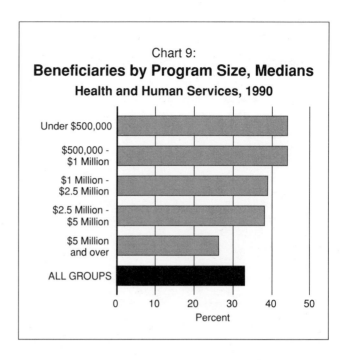

Chart 9:
Beneficiaries by Program Size, Medians
Health and Human Services, 1990

Percent

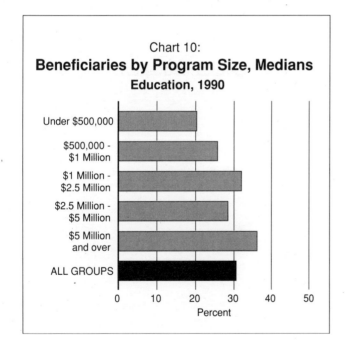

Chart 10:
Beneficiaries by Program Size, Medians
Education, 1990

Percent

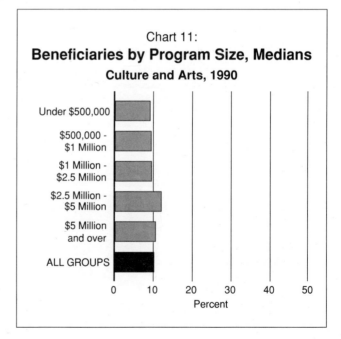

Chart 11:
Beneficiaries by Program Size, Medians
Culture and Arts, 1990

Percent

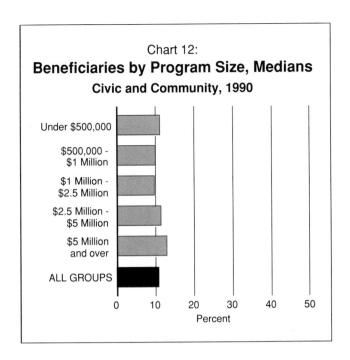

Chart 12:
Beneficiaries by Program Size, Medians
Civic and Community, 1990

Under $500,000

$500,000 -
$1 Million

$1 Million -
$2.5 Million

$2.5 Million -
$5 Million

$5 Million
and over

ALL GROUPS

0 10 20 30 40 50
Percent

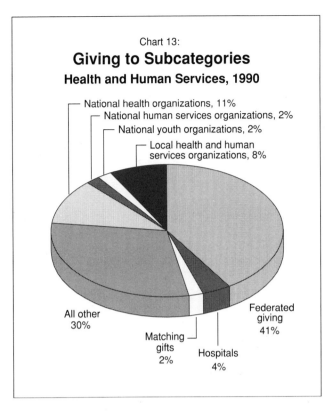

Chart 13:
Giving to Subcategories
Health and Human Services, 1990

National health organizations, 11%
National human services organizations, 2%
National youth organizations, 2%
Local health and human
services organizations, 8%

All other
30%

Matching
gifts
2%

Hospitals
4%

Federated
giving
41%

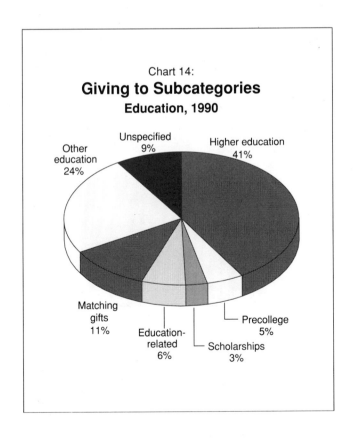

Chart 14:
Giving to Subcategories
Education, 1990

Unspecified
9%

Other
education
24%

Higher education
41%

Matching
gifts
11%

Education-
related
6%

Scholarships
3%

Precollege
5%

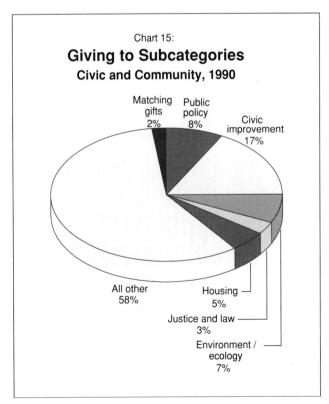

Chart 15:
Giving to Subcategories
Civic and Community, 1990

Matching
gifts
2%

Public
policy
8%

Civic
improvement
17%

All other
58%

Housing
5%

Justice and law
3%

Environment /
ecology
7%

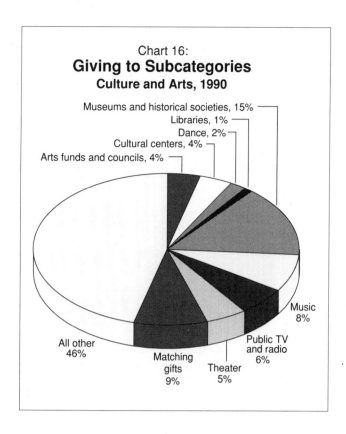

Chart 16:
Giving to Subcategories
Culture and Arts, 1990

Museums and historical societies, 15%
Libraries, 1%
Dance, 2%
Cultural centers, 4%
Arts funds and councils, 4%

Music 8%

Public TV and radio 6%

Theater 5%

Matching gifts 9%

All other 46%

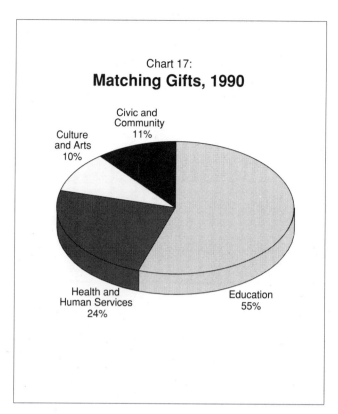

Chart 17:
Matching Gifts, 1990

Civic and Community 11%

Culture and Arts 10%

Health and Human Services 24%

Education 55%

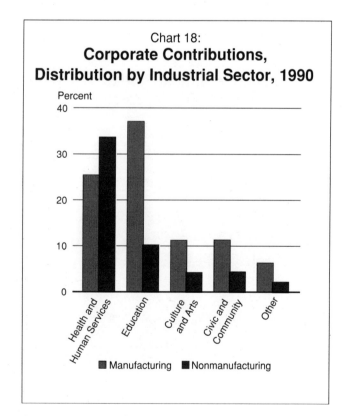

Chart 18:
Corporate Contributions, Distribution by Industrial Sector, 1990

Percent

■ Manufacturing ■ Nonmanufacturing

Health and Human Services

Education

Culture and Arts

Civic and Community

Other

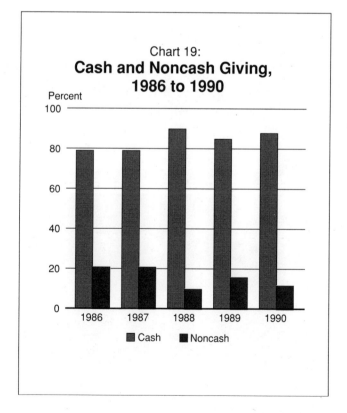

Chart 19:
Cash and Noncash Giving, 1986 to 1990

Percent

1986 1987 1988 1989 1990

■ Cash ■ Noncash

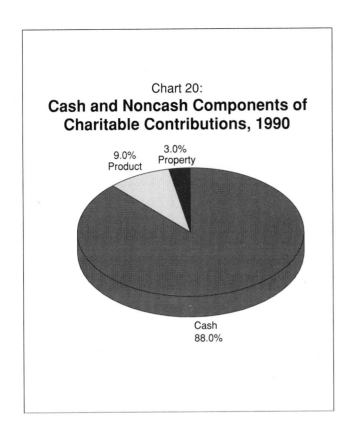

Chart 20:
Cash and Noncash Components of Charitable Contributions, 1990

9.0% Product

3.0% Property

Cash 88.0%

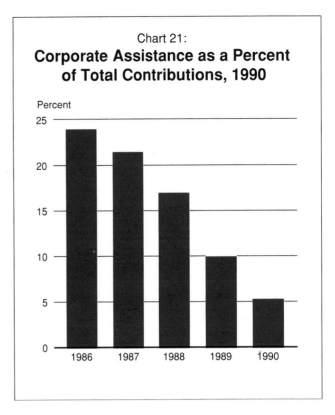

Chart 21:
Corporate Assistance as a Percent of Total Contributions, 1990

Percent

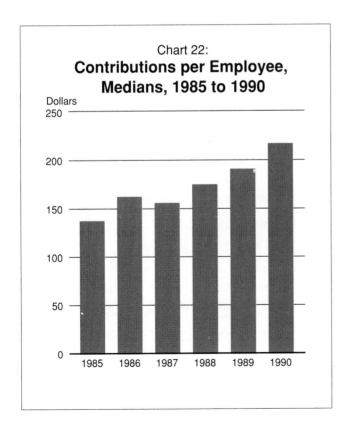

Chart 22:
Contributions per Employee, Medians, 1985 to 1990

Dollars

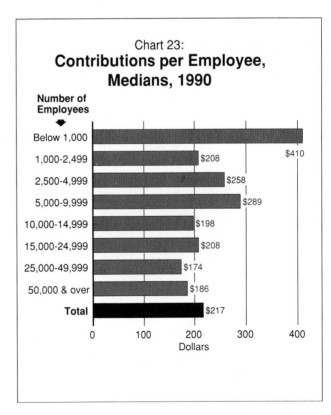

Chart 23:
Contributions per Employee, Medians, 1990

Number of Employees

Below 1,000	$410
1,000-2,499	$208
2,500-4,999	$258
5,000-9,999	$289
10,000-14,999	$198
15,000-24,999	$208
25,000-49,999	$174
50,000 & over	$186
Total	$217

Dollars

Chart 24:
Federated Campaigns Contributions as a Percentage of Total Giving, 1990

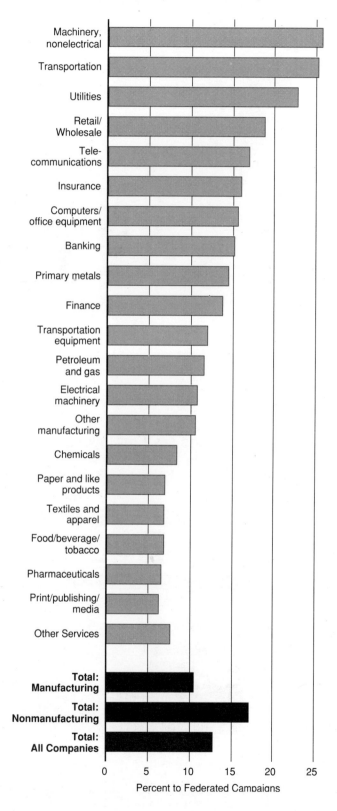

Percent to Federated Campaigns

Chart 25:
Federated Campaigns Contributions per Employee, Medians, 1990

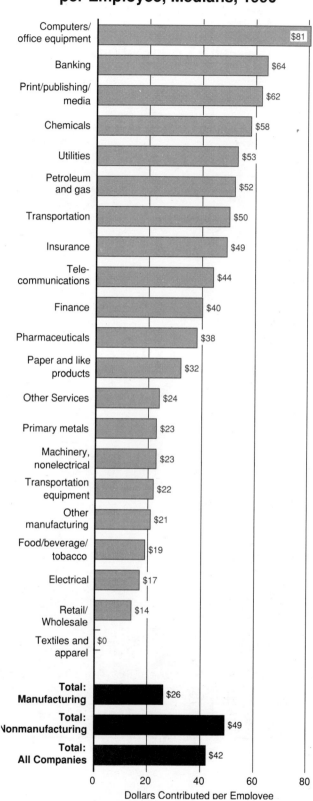

Dollars Contributed per Employee

Chart 26:
Anticipated Changes in 1990
Budgets, Medians

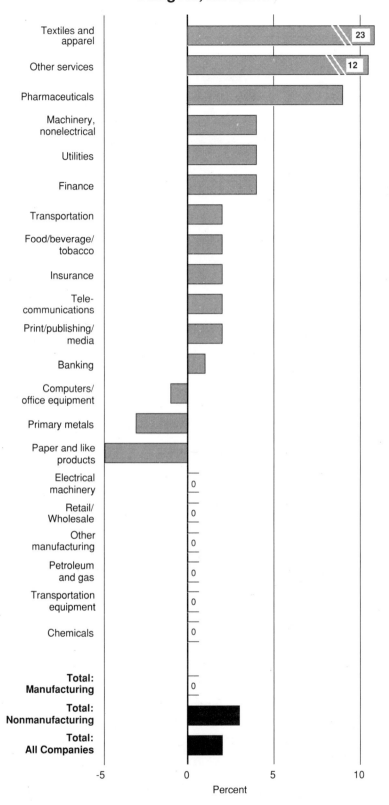

Tables

Table 1: All Corporate Contributions and Corporate Income Before and After Taxes, 1936 to 1990[1]

Year	Contributions ($ Millions)	Income[4] Before Taxes ($ Millions)	Contributions as Percent of Income Before Taxes	Income[4] After Taxes ($ Millions)	Contributions as Percent of Income After Taxes
1936	$ 30	$ 7,900	0.38%	$ 4,900	0.61%
1937	33	7,900	0.42	5,300	0.62
1938	27	4,100	0.65	2,900	0.93
1939	31	7,200	0.43	5,700	0.54
1940	38	10,000	0.38	7,200	0.53
1941	58	17,900	0.32	10,300	0.56
1942	98	21,700	0.45	10,300	0.95
1943	159	25,300	0.63	11,200	1.42
1944	234	24,200	0.97	11,300	2.07
1945	266	19,800	1.34	9,100	2.92
1946	214	24,800	0.86	15,700	1.36
1947	241	31,800	0.76	20,500	1.18
1948	239	35,600	0.67	23,200	1.03
1949	223	29,200	0.76	19,000	1.17
1950	252	42,900	0.59	25,000	1.01
1951	343	44,500	0.77	21,900	1.57
1952	399	39,600	1.01	20,200	1.98
1953	495	41,200	1.20	20,900	2.37
1954	314	38,700	0.81	21,100	1.49
1955	415	49,200	0.84	27,200	1.53
1956	418	49,600	0.84	27,600	1.51
1957	419	48,100	0.87	26,700	1.57
1958	395	41,900	0.94	22,900	1.72
1959	482	52,600	0.92	28,900	1.67
1960	482	49,800	0.97	27,100	1.78
1961	512	49,700	1.03	26,900	1.90
1962	595	55,000	1.08	31,100	1.91
1963	657	59,600	1.10	33,400	1.97
1964	729	66,500	1.10	38,500	1.89
1965	785	77,200	1.02	46,300	1.70
1966	805	83,000	0.97	49,400	1.63
1967	830	79,700	1.04	47,200	1.76
1968	1,005	88,500	1.13	49,400	2.03
1969	1,055	86,700	1.22	47,200	2.24
1970	797	76,000	1.05	41,700	1.91
1971	865	87,300	0.99	49,500	1.75
1972	1,009	101,500	0.99	59,600	1.69
1973	1,174	127,200	0.92	77,900	1.51
1974	1,200	138,900	0.86	87,100	1.38
1975	1,202	134,800	0.89	83,900	1.43
1976	1,487	170,300	0.87	106,000	1.40
1977	1,791	200,500	0.89	127,400	1.41
1978	2,084	233,500	0.89	150,000	1.39
1979	2,288	257,200	0.89	169,300	1.35
1980	2,359	237,100	0.99	152,300	1.55
1981	2,514	226,500	1.11	145,400	1.73
1982	2,906	169,600	1.71	106,500	2.73
1983	3,627	207,600	1.75	130,400	2.78
1984	4,057	239,900	1.69	146,100	2.78
1985	4,472	224,300	1.99	127,900	3.50
1986	5,179 [2]	221,600	2.34	115,300	4.49
1987	4,980	275,300	1.81	148,400	3.36
1988	4,893	316,700	1.54	180,500	2.71
1989	5,800(est.)[3]	307,700	1.88	172,600	3.36
1990	$6,000(est.)[3]	$304,700	1.97	$172,600	3.48

[1] Reflects total consolidated corporate income before and after taxes.

[2] The IRS figure includes some 1987 gifts reported in 1986 to take advantage of the more favorable provisions of the tax law prevailing before the Tax Reform Act of 1986.

[3] IRS figures (1936-1988) are based on direct corporate contributions and corporate gifts to their company foundations. Council for Aid to Eductation estimates (1989 and 1990) reflect direct corporate contributions and gifts by company foundations. Also included in the estimates are carryforwards and returns for companies with noncalendar fiscal years.

[4] The income figures on this table have been adjusted to coincide with recently updated data issued by the Department of Commerce. Thus, some of the figures in the income columns, and the ratios based upon them, will differ slightly from those published here previously.

Note: Figures in this table reflect contributions and income of **all** U.S. corporations. Figures in all other tables in this report are based solely on responses by survey participants.

Sources: Department of Commerce, Internal Revenue Service, Council for Aid to Education.

Table 2A: Contributions as a Percent of U.S. Pretax Income, 1990

Grouped by Industry Class[1]

Industrial Classification	Number of Companies	U.S. Pretax Income (Sum) ($ Thousands)	Contributions (Sum) ($ Thousands)	U.S. Pretax Income (Median) ($ Thousands)	Contributions (Median) ($ Thousands)	Contributions as a Percent of US Pretax Income (Median)
Chemicals	12	$ 6,103,099	$ 123,699	$ 275,500	$ 4,273	1.7%
Computers/office equipment	2	8,256,000	130,189	4,128,000	65,095	4.1
Food/beverage/tobacco	7	5,998,963	71,406	92,429	4,164	1.1
Machinery, nonelectrical	4	306,561	29,981	29,916	423	1.2
Paper and like products	5	815,471	19,423	141,300	4,623	3.4
Petroleum and gas[2]	11	7,901,932	125,631	148,000	3,249	1.5
Pharmaceuticals	8	6,926,880	155,470	854,500	20,872	1.2
Primary metals	2	218,544	2,537	109,272	1,269	1.8
Transportation equipment[3]	6	2,737,272	79,255	378,350	9,997	3.1
Other manufacturing[4]	27	1,807,796	18,212	119,000	1,519	0.9
Total: Manufacturing	66	$ 41,068,518	$ 728,826	$ 180,600	$ 4,140	1.6%
Banking	24	5,763,940	76,155	141,200	1,728	1.9
Finance	2	933,600	24,337	466,800	12,168	2.2
Insurance	20	22,401,386	47,276	154,712	1,125	0.8
Retail and wholesale trade	6	1,828,684	57,766	144,480	2,789	2.3
Telecommunications	10	37,346,356	91,799	665,408	5,448	0.9
Transportation	5	1,521,095	15,160	106,975	1,554	0.9
Utilities	31	12,389,786	48,651	300,417	1,354	0.5
Total: Nonmanufacturing	98	$ 82,184,848	$ 361,148	$ 195,200	$ 1,600	0.8%
Total: All Companies	164	$123,253,366	$1,089,974	$ 193,000	$ 1,909	1.2%

[1] Loss companies excluded.

[2] Includes mining companies.

[3] Includes tire manufacturers.

[4] Includes fabricated metal products; stone, clay and glass products; electrical machinery (not computer); textiles and apparel; and print/publishing/media.

Table 2B: Contributions as a Percent of Worldwide Pretax Income, 1990

Grouped by Industry Class [1]

Industrial Classification	Number of Companies	Worldwide Pretax Income (Sum) ($ Thousands)	Contributions (Sum) ($ Thousands)	Worldwide Pretax Income (Median) ($ Thousands)	Contributions (Median) ($ Thousands)	Contributions as a Percent of Worldwide Pretax Income (Median)
Chemicals	20	$ 14,787,725	$ 157,856	$ 292,106	$ 2,922	0.9%
Computers/office equipment	7	13,028,136	176,897	474,900	6,522	1.6
Electrical machinery (not computer)	10	10,227,161	78,422	308,932	3,874	1.0
Food/beverage/tobacco	13	11,900,374	116,234	188,259	4,164	1.1
Machinery, nonelectrical	8	2,221,335	18,595	261,850	1,742	0.7
Paper and like products	10	2,910,778	40,675	225,399	4,112	1.4
Petroleum and gas[2]	21	29,938,715	205,851	390,000	4,880	0.8
Pharmaceuticals	12	18,713,950	198,247	1,600,500	15,585	1.1
Primary metals	8	1,915,640	16,552	109,259	479	0.8
Printing/publishing/media	6	2,126,629	23,293	297,007	3,474	1.2
Transportation equipment[3]	13	836,246	143,074	402,000	8,993	2.0
Other manufacturing[4]	19	4,260,674	39,554	83,700	1,048	0.9
Total: Manufacturing	147	$120,393,573	$1,215,249	$ 282,506	$ 3,873	1.0%
Banking	32	10,332,189	95,325	150,962	1,584	1.5
Finance	4	2,242,526	30,897	437,413	3,280	0.8
Insurance	15	3,743,180	55,884	170,916	2,375	0.9
Retail and wholesale trade	13	605,357	128,131	260,000	4,612	2.1
Telecommunications	13	16,300,056	162,380	1,317,000	8,146	0.9
Transportation	10	3,063,909	38,311	137,776	1,789	1.2
Utilities	33	12,996,630	57,225	289,200	1,354	0.5
Other services[5]	7	860,018	9,184	107,220	1,242	1.0
Total: Nonmanufacturing	127	$ 55,592,086	$ 577,337	$ 208,742	$ 1,805	0.9%
Total: All Companies	274	$175,985,659	$1,792,586	$ 260,995	$ 2,577	1.0%

[1] Loss companies excluded.
[2] Includes mining companies.
[3] Includes tire manufacturers.
[4] Includes fabricated metal products; stone, clay and glass products; and textiles & apparel.
[5] Includes engineering and construction companies.

Table 3: Beneficiaries of Corporate Support, 1986 to 1990

	1990 330 Companies Thousands of Dollars	% of Total	1989 333 Companies Thousands of Dollars	% of Total	1988 356 Companies Thousands of Dollars	% of Total	1987 325 Companies Thousands of Dollars	% of Total	1986 370 Companies Thousands of Dollars	% of Total
Health and Human Services										
Federated giving	$ 262,628	12.8%	$ 218,250	11.9%	$ 234,045	14.2%	$ 203,582	12.3%	$ 225,944	13.5%
National health organizations	8,660	0.4								
National human services organizations	11,688	0.6								
National youth organizations	14,721	0.7								
Hospitals	25,859	1.3	33,298	1.8	35,249	2.1	31,071	1.9	27,620	1.6
Local health and human services	52,812	2.6								
Matching gifts to health and human services	11,510	0.6	7,024	0.4	10,283	0.6	4,439	0.3	5,527	0.3
All other health and human services	191,931	9.4	222,402	12.2	200,614	12.2	211,423	12.7	209,599	12.5
Total health and human services	$ 580,209	28.3%	$ 480,974	26.4%	$ 480,191	29.2%	$ 450,515	27.2%	$ 468,650	28.0%
Education										
Unrestricted institutional operating grants	$ 57,353	2.8%								
Student financial aid funded through college	25,287	1.2								
General department grants	64,546	3.1								
Project or research grants	47,803	2.3								
Capital grants	35,555	1.7								
Grants to state and national fund raising groups	12,431	0.6								
Matching gifts to higher education	105,458	5.1								
Unspecified for higher education	62,040	3.0								
Total higher education	$ 410,473	20.0%	$ 318,373	17.5%	$ 275,545	16.7%	$ 290,873	17.5%	$ 400,405	23.9%
Preschool	$ 2,684	0.1%								
Public schools	29,747	1.5								
Private schools	2,731	0.1								
Matching gifts to precollege	7,400	0.4								
Unspecified for precollege	14,380	0.7								
Total precollege	$ 56,941	2.8%	$ 53,200	2.9%	$ 41,591	2.5%	$ 25,232	1.5%	$ 30,873	1.8%
Scholarships and fellowships	$ 27,763	1.4%	$ 36,252	1.9%	$ 43,681	2.7%	$ 39,934	2.4%	$ 37,145	2.2%
Education-related organizations	9,647	0.5								
All other organizations	22,601	1.1								
Total for education-related organizations	$ 32,248	1.6%	$ 40,468	2.2%	$ 55,874	3.4%	$ 33,779	2.0%	$ 30,688	1.8%
All other education	$ 246,743	12.0%	$ 136,504	7.5%	$ 89,169	5.4%	$ 112,072	6.7%	$ 111,436	6.7%
Unspecified matching gifts to education	$ 15,011	0.7%	$ 114,984	6.3%	$ 108,190	6.6%	$ 108,257	6.5%	$ 107,436	6.4%
Total education	$ 789,179	38.5%	$ 699,781	38.4%	$ 614,050	37.3%	$ 610,146	36.8%	$ 717,983	42.9%
Culture and Arts										
Arts funds and councils	$ 8,581	0.4%								
Cultural centers	10,126	0.5								
Dance	5,112	0.2								
Libraries	2,119	0.1								
Museums and historical societies	37,603	1.8								
Music	20,116	1.0								
Public TV and radio	14,596	0.7								
Theater	11,835	0.6								
Matching gifts to culture and arts	21,886	1.1	20,004	1.1	18,209	1.1	13,601	0.8	14,782	0.9
All other culture and arts	111,388	5.4	181,199	10.0	165,384	10.0	165,004	9.9	183,972	11.0
Total culture and arts	$ 243,605	11.9%	$ 201,203	11.1%	$ 183,592	11.2%	$ 178,605	10.8%	$ 198,754	11.9%
Civic and Community										
Community improvement	$ 43,041	2.1%	$ 87,009	4.7%	$ 51,335	3.1%	$ 53,356	3.2%	$ 72,622	4.3%
Environment and ecology	18,710	0.9	11,710	0.6	17,349	1.1	44,026	2.7	35,953	2.1
Housing	12,094	0.6	10,238	0.6	9,876	0.6	6,395	0.4	8,237	0.5
Justice and law	8,426	0.4	4,744	0.3	5,711	0.3	6,808	0.4	7,033	0.4
Public policy organizations	20,074	1.0	25,601	1.4	20,918	1.3	22,004	1.3	15,711	0.9
Matching gifts to civic and community	4,016	0.2	12,790	0.7						
All other civic and community	147,811	7.2	101,426	5.5	106,922	6.5	103,536	6.2	80,833	4.8
Total civic and community	$ 254,539	12.4%	$ 253,518	13.9%	$ 212,111	12.9%	$ 236,124	14.2%	$ 220,479	13.2%
Other										
Other (e.g. CARE)	$ 58,188	2.8%								
Unspecified matching gifts	88,712	4.3								
Total other	$ 146,900	7.2%	$ 140,062	7.6%	$ 118,414	7.2	$ 182,992	11.0%	$ 68,119	4.1%
Unspecified	$ 37,037	1.8%	$ 44,538	2.4%	$ 37,331	2.3%				
Grand total	$2,051,469		$1,820,077		$1,645,689		$1,658,382		$1,673,985	

Subcategories may not add to totals due to rounding.

Table 4: Comparison of Corporate Contributions, 1989 and 1990

233 Companies Reporting in Both Years

Beneficiary	1990 Median Contributions Expenditure	1990 Contributions to Beneficiary as Percent of Total Contributions (Median)	1989 Median Contributions Expenditure	1989 Contributions to Beneficiary as Percent of Total Contributions (Median)	Median Percent Change 1989-1990
Health and Human Services	$ 836,495	33.8%	$ 814,543	33.7%	2.9%
Education.............................	864,698	32.8	818,852	31.3	6.1
Culture and Art	317,500	10.4	256,163	10.0	3.8
Civic and Community	255,425	10.6	309,000	11.3	3.7
Other	45,008	1.4	31,657	1.2	38.8
Total	$2,863,884	*	$2,914,103	*	5.0

*Since subcategory percentages are medians rather than sums, they do not add to 100 percent.

Table 5: Health and Human Services Beneficiaries of Company Support, 1990

Companies Grouped by Industry Class

Industrial Classification	Number of Companies	Total Contributions ($ Thousands)	Federated Giving ($ Thousands)	Federated Giving Percent of Industry Contribution	National Health Organizations ($ Thousands)	National Health Organizations Percent of Industry Contribution	National Human Services Organizations ($ Thousands)	National Human Services Organizations Percent of Industry Contribution	National Youth Organizations ($ Thousands)	National Youth Organizations Percent of Industry Contribution	Hospitals ($ Thousands)	Hospitals Percent of Industry Contribution
Chemicals	21	$ 162,379	$ 13,485	8.3%	$ 1,071	0.7%	$806	0.5%	$433	0.3%	$1,583	1.0%
Computers/office equipment	9	196,535	30,499	15.5	1,841	0.9	422	0.2	1,936	1.0	2,593	1.3
Electrical machinery (not computer)	11	79,334	8,474	10.7	23	*	10	*	315	0.4	113	0.1
Food/beverage/tobacco	14	116,644	7,883	6.8	320	0.3	253	0.2	235	0.2	402	0.3
Machinery, nonelectrical	8	18,595	4,801	25.8	211	1.1	85	0.5	521	2.8	184	1.0
Paper and like products	11	56,511	3,876	6.9	179	0.3	344	0.6	281	0.5	276	0.5
Petroleum and gas[1]	22	218,866	25,100	11.5	1,274	0.6	2,370	1.1	2,808	1.3	3,048	1.4
Pharmaceuticals	13	199,491	13,007	6.5	1,094	0.5	2,707	1.4	1,445	0.7	6,906	3.5
Primary metals	11	19,834	2,866	14.4	108	0.5	258	1.3	177	0.9	515	2.6
Print/publishing/media	7	25,852	1,608	6.2	30	0.1	121	0.5	186	0.7	209	0.8
Transportation equipment[2]	17	222,514	26,427	11.9	815	0.4	1,129	0.5	2,001	0.9	3,780	1.7
Other manufacturing[3]	19	39,554	4,701	11.9	54	*	51	*	94	*	404	*
Total: Manufacturing	163	$1,356,110	$142,726	10.5%	$7,020	0.5%	$8,556	0.6%	$10,433	0.8%	$20,013	1.5%
Banking	42	119,549	18,010	15.1	238	0.2	437	0.4	327	0.3	1,504	1.3
Finance	6	35,167	4,802	13.7	2	*	1	*	1	*	248	0.7
Insurance	35	123,789	19,675	15.9	482	0.4	1,101	0.9	541	0.4	1,110	0.9
Retail and Wholesale trade	14	128,930	24,300	18.8	375	0.3	213	0.2	909	0.7	149	0.1
Telecommunications	13	162,380	27,400	16.9	37	*	238	0.1	616	0.4	1,062	0.7
Transportation	10	38,311	9,598	25.1	288	0.8	861	2.2	1,650	4.3	682	1.8
Utilities	36	62,911	14,275	22.7	101	0.2	266	0.4	186	0.3	793	1.3
Other Services[4]	11	24,322	1,842	7.6	96	0.4	14	0.1	60	0.2	298	1.2
Total: Nonmanufacturing	167	$695,359	$119,902	17.2%	$1,620	0.2%	$3,131	0.5%	$4,289	0.6%	$5,846	0.8%
Total: All Companies	330	$2,051,469	$262,628	12.8%	$8,660	0.4%	$11,688	0.6%	$14,721	0.7%	$25,859	1.3%

[1] Includes mining companies.
[2] Includes tire manufacturers.
[3] Includes fabricated metal products; stone, clay, and glass products; and textiles and apparel.
[4] Includes engineering and construction companies.
* Less than 0.1 percent.
Details in row may not add to total due to rounding.

Table 5: Health and Human Services Beneficiaries of Company Support, 1990 (continued)

Industrial Classification	Local Health and Human Services ($ Thousands)	Percent of Industry Contribution	Matching Gifts Health and Human Services ($ Thousands)	Percent of Industry Contribution	All Other Health and Human Services ($ Thousands)	Percent of Industry Contribution	Total Health and Human Services ($ Thousands)	Percent of Industry Contribution
Chemicals	$3,363	2.1%	$110	0.1%	$21,863	13.5%	$42,715	26.3%
Computers/office equipment	2,710	1.4	1,971	1.0	9,791	5.0	51,763	26.3
Electrical machinery (not computer)	884	1.1	1,255	1.6	6,606	8.3	17,680	22.3
Food/beverage/tobacco	1,691	1.4	523	0.4	20,288	17.4	31,595	27.1
Machinery, nonelectrical	935	5.0	429	2.3	487	2.6	7,653	41.2
Paper and like products	1,903	3.4	232	0.4	7,144	12.6	14,235	25.2
Petroleum and gas[1]	5,186	2.4	1,548	0.7	8,313	3.8	49,647	22.7
Pharmaceuticals	3,526	1.8	519	0.3	23,694	11.9	52,900	26.5
Primary metals	1,893	9.5	0	*	354	1.8	6,172	31.1
Print/publishing/media	812	3.1	2,594	10.0	2,833	11.0	8,393	32.5
Transportation equipment[2]	4,271	1.9	58	*	13,485	6.1	51,966	23.4
Other manufacturing[3]	1,397	0.1	116	*	3,836	9.7	10,653	26.9
Total: Manufacturing	$28,571	2.1%	$11,249	0.8%	$118,694	8.8%	$345,371	25.5%
Banking	3,252	2.7	1,070	0.9	12,019	10.1	37,258	31.2
Finance	10	*	461	1.3	3,331	9.5	8,874	25.2
Insurance	4,065	3.3	585	0.5	17,559	14.2	45,117	36.4
Retail and wholesale trade	7,109	5.5	4	*	23,243	18.0	56,301	43.7
Telecommunications	3,891	2.4	0	*	9,047	5.6	42,292	26.0
Transportation	2,862	7.5	20	0.1	1,499	3.9	17,460	45.6
Utilities	2,620	4.2	14	*	6,329	10.1	24,584	39.1
Other services	432	1.8	0	*	211	0.9	2,953	12.1
Total: Nonmanufacturing	$24,241	3.5%	$2,154	0.3%	$73,237	10.5%	$234,838	33.8%
Total: All Companies	$52,812	2.6%	$11,510	0.6%	$191,931	9.4%	$580,209	28.3%

1 Includes mining companies.
2 Includes tire manufacturers.
3 Includes fabricated metal products; stone, clay, and glass products; and textiles and apparel.
4 Includes engineering and construction companies.
* Less than 0.1 percent.
Details in row many not add to total due to rounding.

Table 6: Education Beneficiaries of Company Support, 1990

Companies Grouped by Industry Class

Industrial Classification	Number of Companies	Total Contributions ($Thousands)	Unrestricted Institutional Operating Grants ($ Thousands)	Percent of Industry Contribution	Student Financial Aid Funded Through College or University ($ Thousands)	Percent of Industry Contribution	General Department Grants ($ Thousands)	Percent of Industry Contribution	Project or Research Grants ($ Thousands)	Percent of Industry Contribution	Capital Grants ($ Thousands)	Percent of Industry Contributions	Grants to State/National Fund Raising Groups ($ Thousands)	Percent of Industry Contribution
Chemicals	21	$162,379	$12,459	7.7%	$2,694	1.7%	$5,166	3.2%	$6,033	3.7%	$2,132	1.3%	$503	0.3%
Computers/office equipment	9	196,535	17,302	8.8	817	0.4	31,313	15.9	5,253	2.7	1,000	0.5	914	0.5
Electrical machinery (not computer)	11	79,334	533	0.7	34	*	1,993	2.5	486	0.6	188	0.2	283	0.4
Food/beverage/tobacco	14	116,644	1,987	1.7	63	0.1	266	0.2	498	0.4	1,902	1.6	2,192	1.9
Machinery, nonelectrical	8	18,595	1,179	6.3	226	1.2	184	1.0	498	2.7	544	2.9	64	0.3
Paper and like products [1]	11	56,511	1,189	2.1	493	0.9	716	1.3	346	0.6	405	0.7	195	0.3
Petroleum and gas [1]	22	218,866	3,526	1.6	5,340	2.4	14,692	6.7	6,195	2.8	5,248	2.4	970	0.4
Pharmaceuticals	13	199,491	1,666	0.8	4,885	2.4	1,742	0.9	10,331	5.2	2,257	1.1	1,620	0.8
Primary metals	11	19,834	183	1.0	716	4.0	562	2.8	524	2.6	1,636	8.3	95	0.5
Print/publishing/media	7	25,852	84	0.3	377	1.0	1,112	4.3	150	0.6	40	0.2	97	0.4
Transportation equipment [2]	17	222,514	7,183	3.0	1,828	1.0	562	2.8	4,817	2.2	10,746	4.8	1,772	0.8
Other manufacturing [3]	19	39,554	316	1.0	385	1.0	3,350	8.5	513	1.3	1,145	3.5	103	0.3
Total: Manufacturing	163	$1,356,110	$112,239	8.3%	$17,858	1.3%	$59,530	4.4%	$35,644	2.6%	$27,244	2.0%	$8,809	0.6%
Banking	42	119,549	1,063	0.9	521	0.4	309	0.3	720	0.6	2,025	1.7	717	0.6
Finance	6	35,167	363	1.0	96	0.3	0	*	0	*	0	*	6	*
Insurance	35	123,789	3,762	3.0	910	0.7	614	0.5	201	0.2	2,068	1.7	1,011	0.8
Retail and wholesale trade	14	128,930	175	0.1	534	0.4	561	0.4	470	0.4	853	0.7	479	0.4
Telecommunications	13	162,380	662	0.4	4,496	2.8	215	0.1	5,751	3.5	2,012	1.2	859	0.5
Transportation	10	38,311	1,448	3.8	506	1.3	418	1.1	350	0.9	398	1.0	269	0.7
Utilities [4]	36	62,911	1,747	2.8	326	0.5	554	0.9	195	0.3	590	0.9	247	0.4
Other services [4]	11	24,322	525	2.2	41	0.2	778	3.2	2,654	10.9	365	1.5	36	0.1
Total: Nonmanufacturing	167	$ 695,359	$ 9,744	0.5 %	$ 7,429	0.4 %	$ 3,449	0.2%	$10,341	0.5 %	$ 8,311	0.4%	$ 3,623	0.2%
Total: All Companies	330	$2,051,469	$57,353	2.8%	$25,287	1.2%	$64,546	3.1%	$47,803	2.3%	$35,555	1.7%	$12,431	0.6%

1 Includes mining companies.
2 Includes tire manufacturers.
3 Includes fabricated metal products; stone, clay and glass products; textiles and apparel.
4 Includes engineering and construction companies.
* Less than 0.1 percent.
Details in row may not add to total due to rounding.

Table 6: Education Beneficiaries of Company Support, 1990 (continued)

Industrial Classification	Matching gifts Higher Education ($ Thousands)	Percent of Industry Contribution	Unspecified Higher Education ($ Thousands)	Percent of Industry Contribution	Total Higher Education ($ Thousands)	Percent of Industry Contribution	Preschool ($ Thousands)	Percent of Industry Contribution	Public Schools (K-12) ($ Thousands)	Percent of Industry Contribution	Private Schools (K-12) ($ Thousands)	Percent of Industry Contribution
Chemicals	$5,209	3.2%	$726	0.4%	$34,923	21.5%	$0	*%	$1,304	0.8%	$256	0.2%
Computers/office equipment	13,236	6.7	4,135	2.1	73,970	37.6	104	0.1	2,832	1.4	257	0.1
Electrical machinery (not computer)	5,194	6.5	8,052	10.1	16,763	21.1	0	*	769	1.0	0	*
Food/beverage/tobacco	1,051	0.9	0	*	7,958	6.8	0	*	164	0.1	7	*
Machinery, nonelectrical	964	5.2	0	*	3,660	19.7	40	0.2	138	0.7	17	0.1
Paper and like products	1,304	2.3	0	*	4,648	8.2	177	0.3	1,943	3.4	31	0.1
Petroleum and gas [1]	22,972	10.5	0	*	58,944	26.9	255	0.1	6,218	2.8	510	0.2
Pharmaceuticals	5,180	2.6	1,932	1.0	29,611	14.8	78	*	631	0.3	187	0.1
Primary metals	1,769	8.9	0	*	5,486	27.7	10	0.1	91	0.5	30	0.1
Print/publishing/media	1,303	5.0	250	1.0	3,412	13.2	0	*	50	0.2	17	0.1
Transportation equipment [2]	9,082	4.1	42,854	19.3	81,141	36.5	0	*	4,140	1.9	224	0.1
Other manufacturing [3]	1,912	5.9	0	*	4,867	15.0	8	*	522	*	5	*
Total: Manufacturing	$69,175	5.1%	$57,949	4.3%	$325,383	24.0%	$672	*%	$18,802	1.4%	$1,539	0.1%
Banking	4,260	3.6	353	0.3	9,968	8.3	45	*	484	0.4	165	0.1
Finance	558	1.6	0	*	1,023	2.9	14	*	1	*	0	*
Insurance	8,610	7.0	0	*	18,993	15.3	1,557	1.3	1,228	1.0	286	0.2
Retail and wholesale trade	834	0.6	0	*	3,905	3.0	2	*	786	0.6	138	0.1
Telecommunications	8,374	5.2	3,671	2.3	26,040	16.0	25	*	3,308	2.0	177	0.1
Transportation	477	1.2	0	*	3,866	10.1	0	*	526	1.4	234	0.6
Utilities	1,234	2.0	67	0.1	4,959	7.9	123	*	125	0.2	184	0.3
Other services [4]	11,937	49.1	0	*	16,336	67.2	244	0.2	122	0.5	8	*
Total: Nonmanufacturing	$ 36,283	1.7%	$ 4,091	0.2%	$ 85,090	4.0%	$2,009	0.3%	$ 6,580	0.9%	$1,192	0.2%
Total: All Companies	$105,458	*%	$62,040	3.0%	$410,473	20.0%	$2,684	0.1%	$29,747	1.5%	$2,731	0.1%

[1] Includes mining companies.
[2] Includes tire manufacturers.
[3] Includes fabricated metal products; stone, clay and glass products; and textiles and apparel.
[4] Includes engineering and construction companies.
* Less than 0.1 percent.
Details in row may not add to total due to rounding.

Table 6: Education Beneficiaries of Company Support, 1990 (continued)

Industrial Classification	Matching Gifts Precollege ($ Thousands)	Percent of Industry Contribution	Unspecified Precollege ($ Thousands)	Percent of Industry Contribution	Total Precollege ($ Thousands)	Percent of Industry Contribution	Scholarships and Fellowships ($ Thousands)	Percent of Industry Contribution	Education Related Organizations ($ Thousands)	Percent of Industry Contribution	All Other Organizations ($ Thousands)	Percent of Industry Contribution
Chemicals	$ 277	0.2%	$691	0.4%	$2,528	1.6%	$1,603	1.0%	$740	0.5%	$3,555	2.2%
Computers/office equipment	645	0.3	2,803	1.4	6,640	3.4	6,513	3.3	474	0.2	1,858	0.9
Electrical machinery (not computer)	74	0.1	294	0.4	3,776	4.8	838	1.1	103	0.1	193	0.2
Food/beverage/tobacco	165	0.1	183	0.2	519	0.4	1,071	0.9	142	0.1	86	0.1
Machinery, nonelectrical	60	0.3	0	*	255	1.4	126	0.7	315	1.7	129	0.7
Paper and like products	236	0.4	0	*	2,389	4.2	437	0.8	232	0.4	161	0.3
Petroleum and gas[1]	1,205	0.6	2,975	1.4	11,163	5.1	2,457	1.1	1,335	0.6	7,577	3.5
Pharmaceuticals	804	0.4	757	0.4	2,456	1.2	2,328	1.2	414	0.2	1,586	0.8
Primary metals	0	*	80	0.4	211	1.1	66	0.3	169	0.9	286	1.4
Print/publishing/media	185	0.7	0	*	252	1.0	570	2.2	60	0.2	260	1.0
Transportation equipment[2]	797	0.4	3,122	1.4	8,284	3.7	469	2.1	2,240	1.0	1,774	0.8
Other manufacturing[3]	310	*	0	*	844	2.6	851	2.6	334	0.3	49	0.2
Total: Manufacturing	$4,759	0.4%	$10,904	0.8%	$39,318	2.9%	$21,559	1.6%	$6,559	0.5%	$17,515	1.3%
Banking	1,610	1.3	184	0.2	6,853	5.7	677	0.6	606	0.5	1,157	1.0
Finance	12	*	301	0.9	327	0.9	77	0.2	77	0.2	0	*
Insurance	731	0.6	294	0.2	4,096	3.3	1,689	1.4	837	0.7	1,147	0.9
Retail and wholesale trade	29	*	44	*	999	0.8	478	0.4	301	0.2	555	0.4
Telecommunications	82	0.1	0	*	3,592	2.2	589	0.4	308	0.2	2,039	1.3
Transportation	93	0.2	0	*	85	0.2	1,436	3.7	862	2.2	125	0.3
Utilities	74	0.1	14	*	521	0.8	454	0.7	245	0.4	15	*
Other services[4]	9	*	0	*	383	1.6	802	3.3	75	0.3	49	0.2
Total: Nonmanufacturing	$2,641	0.4%	$ 837	0.1%	$16,857	0.8%	$ 6,203	0.3%	$3,312	0.2%	$5,086	0.2%
Total: All Companies	$7,400	0.4%	$14,380	0.7%	$56,941	2.8%	$27,763	1.4%	$9,647	0.5%	$22,601	1.1%

[1] Includes mining companies.
[2] Includes tire manufacturers.
[3] Includes fabricated metal products; stone, clay and glass products; and textiles and apparel.
[4] Includes engineering and construction companies.
* Less than 0.1 percent.
Details in row may not add to total due to rounding.

Table 6: Education Beneficiaries of Company Support, 1990 (continued)

Industrial Classification	Total Education-Related Organization ($ Thousands)	Percent of Industry Contribution	Unspecified Matching Gifts Education ($ Thousands)	Percent of Industry Contribution	Total Education ($ Thousands)	Percent of Industry Contribution
Chemicals	$5,899	3.6%	$685	0.4%	$7,457	4.6%
Computers/office equipment	8,845	4.4	0	*	94,950	48.3
Electrical machinery (not computer)	1,134	1.4	0	*	28,610	36.1
Food/beverage/tobacco	1,299	1.1	740	0.6	36,301	31.1
Machinery, nonelectrical	571	3.1	26	0.1	6,351	34.2
Paper and like products	830	1.5	315	0.6	21,112	37.4
Petroleum and gas [1]	11,369	5.2	1,623	0.7	99,964	45.7
Pharmaceuticals	4,328	2.2	2,368	1.2	65,667	32.9
Primary metals	522	2.6	47	0.2	8,260	41.6
Print/publishing/media	890	3.4	185	0.7	8,703	33.7
Transportation equipment [2]	8,712	3.9	1,680	0.8	469	52.4
Other manufacturing [3]	1,011	3.1	400	1.2	11,085	28.0
Total: Manufacturing	$45,410	3.3%	$8,068	0.6%	$505,079	37.2%
Banking	2,440	2.0	3,440	2.9	35,317	29.5
Finance	154	0.4	107	0.3	10,926	31.1
Insurance	3,673	3.0	373	0.3	36,140	29.2
Retail and wholesale trade	1,333	1.0	29	*	18,189	14.1
Telecommunications	2,936	1.8	2,560	1.6	74,885	46.1
Transportation	2,423	6.3	0	*	8,086	21.1
Utilities	715	1.1	433	0.7	14,720	23.4
Other services [4]	927	3.8	0	*	18,746	77.1
Total: Nonmanufacturing	$14,601	0.7%	$6,943	0.3%	$217,010	10.3%
Total: All Companies	$60,011	2.9%	$15,011	0.7%	$789,179	38.5%

[1] Includes mining companies.
[2] Includes tire manufacturers.
[3] Includes fabricated metal products: stone, clay and glass products; and textiles and apparel.
[4] Includes engineering and construction companies.
* Less than 0.1 percent.
Details in row may not add to total due to rounding.

Table 7: Culture and Arts Beneficiaries of Company Support, 1990

Companies Grouped by Industry Class

Industrial Classification	Number of Companies	Total Contributions ($Thousands)	Arts Funds and Councils ($ Thousands)	Percent of Industry Contribution	Cultural Centers ($ Thousands)	Percent of Industry Contribution	Dance ($ Thousands)	Percent of Industry Contribution	Libraries ($ Thousands)	Percent of Industry Contribution	Museums ($ Thousands)	Percent of Industry Contribution	Music ($Thousands)	Percent of Industry Contribution
Chemicals	21	$162,379	$394	0.2%	$366	0.2%	$110	0.1%	$283	0.2%	$2,457	1.5%	$1,962	1.2%
Computers/office equipment	9	196,535	1,335	0.7	13	*	120	0.1	111	0.1	7,919	4.0	414	0.2
Electrical machinery (not computer)	11	79,334	66	0.1	306	0.4	155	0.2	46	0.1	335	0.4	359	0.5
Food/beverage/tobacco	14	116,644	203	0.2	35	*	73	0.1	7	*	723	0.6	624	0.5
Machinery, nonelectrical	8	18,595	24	0.1	17	0.1	3	*	77	0.4	235	1.3	168	0.9
Paper and like products	11	56,511	316	0.6	563	1.0	28	*	92	0.2	912	1.6	94	0.2
Petroleum and gas[1]	22	218,866	1,993	0.9	2,633	1.2	619	0.3	465	0.2	4,375	2.0	3,737	1.7
Pharmaceuticals	13	199,491	192	0.1	743	0.4	130	0.1	122	0.1	1,849	0.9	1,267	0.6
Primary metals	11	19,834	109	0.5	116	0.6	0	*	71	0.4	598	3.0	345	1.7
Print/publishing/media[2]	7	25,852	60	0.2	133	0.5	34	0.1	140	0.5	348	1.3	122	0.5
Transportation equipment[3]	17	222,514	51	*	398	0.2	493	0.2	112	0.1	469	2.6	1,135	0.5
Other manufacturing[4]	19	39,554	743	1.9	62	0.2	57	0.2	51	0.2	3,167	9.8	122	0.4
Total: Manufacturing	163	$1,356,110	$5,484	0.4%	$5,384	0.4%	$1,821	0.1%	$1,574	0.1%	$28,611	2.1%	$10,348	0.8%
Banking	42	119,549	484	0.4	1,073	0.9	417	0.3	233	0.2	2,064	1.7	1,539	1.3
Finance	6	35,167	0	*	208	0.6	179	0.5	0	*	597	1.7	742	2.1
Insurance	35	123,789	881	0.7	947	0.8	641	0.5	176	0.1	10,615	8.6	754	0.6
Retail and wholesale trade	14	128,930	707	0.5	329	0.3	980	0.8	38	*	2,792	2.2	3,552	2.8
Telecommunications	13	162,380	320	0.2	1,255	0.8	801	0.5	13	*	958	0.6	1,419	0.9
Transportation	10	38,311	379	1.0	327	0.9	102	0.3	3	*	814	2.1	962	2.5
Utilities	36	62,911	202	0.3	260	0.4	39	0.1	81	0.1	620	1.0	724	1.2
Other services[4]	11	24,322	181	0.7	342	1.4	38	0.2	1	*	86	0.4	77	0.3
Total: Nonmanufacturing	167	$695,359	$3,154	0.1%	$4,741	0.2%	$3,197	0.2%	$544	*%	$18,546	*%	$9,768	0.5%
Total: All Companies	330	$2,051,469	$8,581	0.4%	$10,126	0.5%	$5,112	0.2%	$2,119	0.1%	$37,603	*%	$20,116	1.0%

[1] Includes mining companies.
[2] Includes tire manufacturers.
[3] Includes fabricated metal products; stone, clay and glass products; and textiles and apparel.
[4] Includes engineering and construction companies.
* Less than 0.1 percent.
Details in row may not add to total due to rounding.

Table 7: Culture and Arts Beneficiaries of Company Support, 1990 (continued)

Companies Grouped by Industry Class

Industrial Classification	Public TV and Radio ($ Thousands)	Percent of Industry Contribution	Theater ($ Thousands)	Percent of Industry Contribution	Matching Gifts Culture and Art ($ Thousands)	Percent of Industry Contribution	Unspecified Culture and Art ($ Thousands)	Percent of Industry Contribution	Total Culture and Art ($ Thousands)	Percent of Industry Contribution
Chemicals	$702	0.4%	$807	0.5%	$526	0.3%	$9,244	5.7%	$16,850	10.4%
Computers/office equipment	2,523	1.3	746	0.4	7,141	3.6	1,686	0.9	22,007	11.2
Electrical machinery (not computer)	41	0.1	74	0.1	629	0.8	8,169	10.3	10,178	12.8
Food/beverage/tobacco	2,915	2.5	331	0.3	409	0.4	1,695	1.5	22,303	19.1
Machinery, nonelectrical	220	1.2	16	0.1	280	1.5	661	3.6	1,701	9.1
Paper and like products [1]	335	0.6	349	0.6	249	0.4	3,854	6.8	7,033	12.4
Petroleum and gas [1]	1,436	0.7	1,306	0.6	2,499	1.1	7,128	3.3	26,191	12.0
Pharmaceuticals	1,427	0.7	648	0.3	1,888	0.9	2,610	1.3	10,875	5.5
Primary metals	116	0.6	266	1.3	43	0.2	413	2.1	2,113	10.7
Print/publishing/media	12	*	66	0.3	523	2.0	2,112	8.2	3,601	13.9
Transportation equipment [2]	437	0.2	1,100	0.5	1,536	0.7	469	6.0	24,898	11.2
Other manufacturing [3]	100	0.3	150	0.5	425	1.3	1,299	3.3	5,543	14.0
Total: Manufacturing	$10,264	0.8 %	$5,859	0.4%	$16,148	1.2%	$52,231	3.9%	$153,294	11.3%
Banking	332	0.3	1,094	0.9	1,741	1.5	7,549	6.3	16,526	13.8
Finance	51	0.1	605	1.7	238	0.7	3,065	8.7	5,686	16.2
Insurance	2,019	1.6	336	0.3	814	0.7	5,846	4.7	13,475	10.9
Retail and wholesale trade	1,419	1.1	2,482	1.9	85	0.1	4,674	3.6	17,058	13.2
Telecommunications	82	0.1	1,087	0.7	2,410	1.5	13,967	8.6	22,312	13.7
Transportation	269	0.7	140	0.4	124	0.3	661	1.7	3,780	9.9
Utilities	135	0.2	196	0.3	325	0.5	7,492	11.9	10,074	16.0
Other services [4]	26	0.1	35	0.1	0	*	613	2.5	1,400	5.8
Total: Nonmanufacturing	$4,332	0.2%	$5,976	0.3 %	$5,738	0.3%	$43,867	2.1%	$90,311	4.3%
Total: All Companies	$14,596	0.7%	$11,835	0.6%	$21,886	1.1%	$111,388	5.4%	$243,605	11.9%

[1] Includes mining companies.
[2] Includes tire manufacturers.
[3] Includes fabricated metal products; stone, clay and glass products; and textiles and apparel.
[4] Includes engineering and construction companies.
* Less than 0.1 percent.
Details in row may not add to total due to rounding.

Table 8: Civic and Community Beneficiaries of Company Support, 1990

Companies Grouped by Industry Class

Industrial Classification	Number of Companies	Total Contributions ($ Thousands)	Community Improvement ($ Thousands)	Community Improvement Percent of Industry Contribution	Environment and Ecology ($ Thousands)	Environment and Ecology Percent of Industry Contribution	Housing ($ Thousands)	Housing Percent of Industry Contribution	Justice and Law ($ Thousands)	Justice and Law Percent of Industry Contribution	Public Policy Organizations ($ Thousands)	Public Policy Organizations Percent of Industry Contributions	Matching Gifts Civic and Community ($ Thousands)	Matching Gifts Civic and Community Percent of Industry Contribution
Chemicals	21	$162,379	$3,564	2.2%	$2,798	1.7%	$913	0.6%	$288	0.2%	$773	0.5%	$120	0.1%
Computers/office equipment	9	196,535	2,572	1.3	895	0.5	653	0.3	448	0.2	375	0.2	933	0.5
Electrical machinery (not computer)	11	79,334	173	0.2	117	0.1	9	*	14	*	246	0.3	81	0.1
Food/beverage/tobacco	14	116,644	762	0.7	434	0.4	241	0.2	277	0.2	211	0.2	52	*
Machinery, nonelectrical	8	18,595	923	5.0	5	*	145	0.8	20	0.1	320	1.7	40	0.2
Paper and like products	11	56,511	612	1.1	447	0.8	152	0.3	69	0.1	333	0.6	83	0.1
Petroleum and gas [1]	22	218,866	6,717	3.1	8,956	4.1	2,696	1.2	1,032	0.5	5,204	2.4	591	0.3
Pharmaceuticals	13	199,491	4,900	2.5	416	0.2	474	0.2	444	0.2	3,906	2.0	325	0.2
Primary metals	11	19,834	188	0.9	263	1.3	2	*	46	0.2	351	1.4	94	0.4
Print/publishing/media	7	25,852	211	0.8	53	0.2	0	*	0	*	0	*	0	*
Transportation equipment [2]	17	222,514	7,662	3.4	1,220	0.5	145	0.7	120	0.6	3,376	1.0	0	*
Other manufacturing [3]	19	39,554	1,525	4.7	191	0.6	331	0.8	48	0.1	3,576	9.0	545	1.4
Total: Manufacturing	163	$1,356,110	$29,808	2.2 %	$15,795	1.2 %	$5,762	0.4%	$3,207	0.2 %	$15,615	1.2 %	$2,865	0.2 %
Banking	42	119,549	3,757	3.1	645	0.5	3,718	3.1	256	0.2	1,045	0.9	561	0.5
Finance	6	35,167	395	1.1	2	*	32	0.1	11	*	538	1.5	159	0.5
Insurance	35	123,789	3,328	2.7	243	0.2	1,112	0.9	4,323	3.5	1,729	1.4	410	0.3
Retail and wholesale trade	14	128,930	3,132	2.4	324	0.3	746	0.6	232	0.2	279	0.2	0	*
Telecommunications	13	162,380	7,400	4.6	152	0.1	100	0.1	162	0.1	431	0.3	0	*
Transportation	10	38,311	710	1.9	134	0.3	11	*	61	0.2	358	0.9	0	*
Utilities	36	62,911	999	1.6	1,371	2.2	597	0.9	123	0.2	61	0.1	17	*
Other services [4]	11	24,322	172	0.7	45	0.2	16	0.1	51	0.2	19	0.1	5	*
Total: Nonmanufacturing	167	$695,359	$19,893	0.9 %	$2,915	0.1 %	$6,332	0.3%	$5,219	0.2%	$4,459	0.2 %	$1,152	0.1%
Total: All Companies	330	$2,051,469	$4,301	0.2%	$18,710	0.9%	$12,094	0.6%	$8,426	0.4%	$20,074	1.0%	$4,016	0.2%

[1] Includes mining companies.
[2] Includes tire manufacturers.
[3] Includes fabricated metal products; stone, clay and glass products; and textiles and apparel.
[4] Includes engineering and construction companies.
*Less than 0.1 percent.
Details in row may not add to total due to rounding.

Table 8B: Civic and Community Beneficiaries of Company Support, 1990 (continued)

Industrial Classification	Unspecified ($ Thousands)	Percent of Industry Contribution	Total Civic and Community ($ Thousands)	Percent of Industry Contribution
Chemicals	$10,775	6.6%	$19,230	11.8%
Computers/office equipment	8,229	4.2	14,105	7.2
Electrical machinery (not computer)	6,310	8.0	6,951	8.8
Food/beverage/tobacco	13,172	11.3	15,149	13.0
Machinery, nonelectrical	531	2.9	1,983	10.7
Paper and like products	6,382	11.3	8,444	14.9
Petroleum and gas[1]	11,605	5.3	36,801	16.8
Pharmaceuticals	11,862	5.9	22,327	11.2
Primary metals	1,452	5.6	2,015	10.2
Print/publishing/media	2,072	29.3	2,209	8.5
Transportation equipment[2]	1,097	5.5	23,481	10.6
Other manufacturing[3]	12,460	31.5	6,668	16.8
Total: Manufacturing	$85,945	6.3%	$154,767	11.4%
Banking	10,486	8.8	20,467	17.1
Finance	2,275	6.5	3,411	9.7
Insurance	1,102	0.9	22,170	17.9
Retail and wholesale trade	15,108	11.7	19,818	15.4
Telecommunications	14,132	8.7	15,716	9.7
Transportation	1,138	3.0	2,412	6.3
Utilities	7,000	11.1	10,168	16.2
Other services[4]	707	2.9	1,014	4.2
Total: Nonmanufacturing	$51,948	2.5%	$95,176	4.5%
Total: All Companies	$147,811	7.2%	$254,539	12.4%

[1] Includes mining companies.
[2] Includes tire manufacturers.
[3] Includes fabricated metal products; stone, clay and glass products; and textiles and apparel.
[4] Includes engineering and construction companies.
*Less than 0.1 percent.
Details in row may not add to total due to rounding.

Table 9: "Other" and Unspecified Beneficiaries of Company Support, 1990

Companies Grouped by Industry Class

Industrial Classification	Number of Companies($	Total Contributions (Thousands)	Other ($ Thousands)	Other Percent of Industry Contribution	Unspecified Matching Gifts ($ Thousands)	Unspecified Matching Gifts Percent of Industry Contribution	Total Other ($ Thousands)	Total Other Percent of Industry Contribution	Unspecified ($ Thousands)	Unspecified Percent of Industry Contribution
Chemicals	21	$162,379	$1,611	1.0%	$723	0.4%	$2,334	1.4%	$197	0.1%
Computers/office equipment	9	196,535	8,227	4.2	548	0.3	8,775	4.5	0	*
Electrical machinery (not computer)	11	79,334	12,061	15.2	1,737	2.2	13,798	17.4	2,118	2.7
Food/beverage/tobacco	14	116,644	890	0.8	6,605	5.7	7,495	6.4	3,801	3.3
Machinery, nonelectrical	8	18,595	37	0.2	864	4.6	901	4.8	5	*
Paper and like products	11	56,511	265	0.5	3,842	6.8	4,107	7.3	158	0.3
Petroleum and gas[1]	22	218,866	1,900	0.9	4,120	1.9	6,020	2.8	242	0.1
Pharmaceuticals	13	199,491	21,630	10.8	6,283	3.1	27,913	14.0	19,810	9.9
Primary metals	11	19,834	339	1.7	936	4.7	1,275	6.4	0	*
Print/publishing/media	7	25,852	151	0.6	2,796	10.8	2,947	11.4	0	*
Transportation equipment[2]	17	222,514	469	1.2	2,804	1.3	5,550	2.5	0	*
Other manufacturing[3]	19	39,554	303	0.9	5,232	13.2	5,535	14.0	71	*
Total: Manufacturing	163	$1,356,110	$50,160	3.7%	$36,490	2.7%	$86,650	6.4%	$26,401	1.9%
Banking	42	119,549	1,952	1.6	7,045	5.9	8,997	7.5	984	0.8
Finance	6	35,167	124	0.4	6,110	17.4	6,233	17.7	36	0.1
Insurance	35	123,789	157	0.1	6,730	5.4	6,887	5.6	0	*
Retail and wholesale trade	14	128,930	2,836	2.2	7,669	5.9	10,505	8.1	7,059	5.5
Telecommunications	13	162,380	2,720	1.7	3,455	2.1	6,175	3.8	1,000	0.6
Transportation	10	38,311	100	0.3	6,474	16.9	6,574	17.2	0	*
Utilities	36	62,911	128	0.2	3,238	5.1	6,574	5.3	0	*
Other services[4]	11	24,322	13	0.1	60	0.2	72	0.3	136	0.6
Total: Nonmanufacturing	167	$ 695,359	$ 8,028	0.4%	$40,781	1.9%	$ 48,809	2.3%	$ 9,215	1.3%
Total: All Companies	330	$2,051,469	$58,188	2.8%	$88,712	4.3%	$146,900	7.2%	$37,037	1.8%

[1] Includes mining companies.

[2] Includes tire manufacturers.

[3] Includes fabricated metal products; stone, clay and glass products; and textiles and apparel.

[4] Includes engineering and construction companies.

*Less than 0.1 percent.

Details in row may not add to total due to rounding.

Table 10: Federated Campaigns, Median Contributions

Program Size	Number of Companies	Median Contribution to Federated Campaigns
Less than $500,000	39	$71,500
$500,000 to $1 million	33	220,900
$1 million to $2.5 million	66	338,022
$2.5 million to $5 million	54	714,400
$5 million and over	81	1,771,000
Total	273	$415,745

Table 11: Cash and Noncash Giving, by Industry, 1990

Industrial Classification	Number of Companies	Total Contributions Cash and Noncash ($ Thousands)	Cash as a Percent of Total Contributions	Securities as a Percent of Total Contributions	Company Product as a Percent of Total Contributions	Property and Equipment as a Percent of Total Contributions
Chemicals	21	$162,379	81%	0%	13%	5%
Computers/office equipment	9	192,935	66	0	29	5
Electrical machinery (not computer)	11	79,334	97	0	2	1
Food/beverage/tobacco	14	116,644	94	0	6	0
Machinery, nonelectrical	8	18,595	100	0	0	0
Paper and like products	11	56,511	80	0	20	1
Petroleum and gas[1]	22	218,866	99	0	0	1
Pharmaceuticals	13	199,491	69	0	31	1
Primary metals	10	17,518	100	0	0	0
Print/publishing/media	7	25,852	83	0	17	0
Transportation equipment[2]	17	215,936	88	0	2	10
Other manufacturing[3]	19	39,544	99	0	0	0
Total: Manufacturing	162	$1,343,615	84%	0%	12%	3%
Banking	43	122,211	100	0	0	0
Finance	6	35,167	100	0	0	0
Insurance	35	123,789	99	0	0	1
Retail and wholesale trade	13	127,330	97	0	1	2
Telecommunications	13	162,380	89	0	10	1
Transportation	11	40,393	94	0	5	1
Utilities	36	62,911	99	0	0	1
Other services[4]	13	31,530	100	0	0	0
Total: Nonmanufacturing	170	$705,712	96%	0%	3%	1%
Total: All Companies	332	$2,049,327	88%	0%	9%	3%

[1] Includes mining companies.

[2] Includes tire manufacturers.

[3] Includes fabricated metal products; stone, clay and glass products; and textiles and apparel.

[4] Includes engineering and construction companies.

Total may not add to 100 percent due to rounding.

Table 12: 75 Top Donors, Contributions as a Percent of U.S. and Worldwide Pretax Income, 1990

Company Rank	Contributions[1] (Dollars)	U.S. Pretax Income[2] ($ Thousands)	Contributions as Percent of U.S. Pretax Income	Worldwide Pretax Income[2] ($ Thousands)	Contributions as Percent of Worldwide Pretax Income
1	$101,400,000	$ 7,844,000	1.3%	$10,203,000	1.0%
2	65,300,000	n.a.	n.a.	*	*
3	51,813,374	n.a.	n.a.	4,229,000	1.2
4	46,637,106	n.a.	n.a.	6,147,000	0.8
5	45,400,000	4,743,000	1.0	6,311,000	0.7
6	37,913,600	2,054,000	1.8	8,065,000	0.5
7	37,200,000	635,000	5.9	1,623,000	2.3
8	36,914,100	885,600	4.2	1,495,000	2.5
9	32,120,700	1,304,000	2.5	1,602,000	2.0
10	31,100,143	1,234,000	2.5	2,134,000	1.5
11	30,731,854	659,000	4.7	659,000	4.7
12	30,667,792	n.a.	n.a.	123,989	24.7
13	29,200,000	1,853,000	1.6	4,154,000	0.7
14	28,789,763	412,000	7.0	1,056,000	2.7
15	26,417,984	1,396,000	1.9	3,410,000	0.8
16	26,335,000	1,767,000	1.5	2,011,000	1.3
17	24,544,913	1,134,600	2.2	1,599,000	1.5
18	23,381,475	n.a.	n.a.	673,000	3.5
19	22,498,084	833,000	2.7	1,257,000	1.8
20	22,354,156	n.a.	n.a.	2,563,000	0.9
21	21,926,694	1,832,500	1.2	2,698,800	0.8
22	21,880,143	609,000	3.6	1,019,000	2.1
23	21,419,115	1,896,000	1.1	4,213,000	0.5
24	21,187,870	265,000	8.0	826,000	2.6
25	21,073,085	n.a.	n.a.	1,544,000	1.4
26	20,801,634	1,823,000	1.1	2,230,000	0.9
27	20,735,302	1,810,600	1.1	1,810,600	1.1
28	20,658,411	832,000	2.5	832,000	2.5
29	20,030,099	n.a.	n.a.	535,300	3.7
30	19,816,454	558,392	3.5	655,550	3.0
31	19,585,000	n.a.	n.a.	1,972,000	1.0
32	18,910,640	n.a.	n.a.	4,444,000	0.4
33	18,101,699	*	*	*	*
34	17,507,606	639,000	2.7	809,000	2.2
35	17,145,000	30,200,000	0.1	1,600,000	1.1
36	16,951,743	n.a.	n.a.	134,000	12.7
37	16,553,936	n.a.	n.a.	2,500,000	0.7
38	16,193,781	n.a.	n.a.	n.a.	n.a.
39	15,962,208	n.a.	n.a.	2,175,000	0.7
40	15,836,352	n.a.	n.a.	n.a.	n.a.
41	15,714,000	1,541,000	1.0	1,541,000	1.0
42	15,700,000	n.a.	n.a.	999,884	1.6
43	15,647,500	561,347	2.8	713,403	2.2
44	15,400,000	n.a.	n.a.	n.a.	n.a.
45	15,290,621	n.a.	n.a.	1,667,400	0.9
46	15,174,891	n.a.	n.a.	1,982,100	0.8
47	14,615,915	1,074,000	1.4	1,351,000	1.1
48	13,400,232	840,000	1.6	1,052,000	1.3
49	13,342,800	n.a.	n.a.	1,352,100	1.0
50	13,015,517	n.a.	n.a.	n.a.	n.a.

[1] Direct giving and company foundation payouts included; grants made to and retained by company foundations are excluded.

[2] U.S. and worldwide pretax income rounded, percentages actual.

*Company showed loss.

n.a.=Not available.

Table 12: 75 Top Donors, Contributions as a Percent of U.S. and Worldwide Pretax Income, 1990 (continued)

Company Rank	Contributions[1] (Dollars)	U.S. Pretax Income[2] ($ Thousands)	Contributions as Percent of U.S. Pretax Income	Worldwide Pretax Income[2] ($ Thousands)	Contributions as Percent of Worldwide Pretax Income
51	$12,175,544	n.a.	n.a.	$ 624,200	2.0%
52	11,701,456	n.a.	n.a.	1,047,200	1.1
53	11,279,000	n.a.	n.a.	2,043,660	0.6
54	11,055,000	n.a.	n.a.	1,050,000	1.1
55	11,050,000	952,000	1.2	952,000	1.2
56	11,001,103	558,700	2.0	1,291,200	0.9
57	10,678,768	n.a.	n.a.	612,700	1.7
58	10,502,374	96,000	10.9	112,000	9.4
59	10,441,940	n.a.	n.a.	*	*
60	10,082,211	n.a.	n.a.	624,000	1.6
61	10,078,882	n.a.	n.a.	n.a.	n.a.
62	9,998,665	n.a.	n.a.	501,000	2.0
63	8,992,573	178,000	5.1	343,000	2.6
64	8,890,797	n.a.	n.a.	428,000	2.1
65	8,725,659	n.a.	n.a.	402,000	2.2
66	8,661,000	n.a.	n.a.	352,000	2.5
67	8,261,874	n.a.	n.a.	946,000	0.9
68	8,261,410	292,000	2.8	1,054,000	0.8
69	8,146,378	164,900	4.9	164,900	4.9
70	8,054,321	n.a.	n.a.	188,000	4.3
71	7,870,000	n.a.	n.a.	n.a.	n.a.
72	7,575,000	n.a.	n.a.	1,176,174	0.6
73	7,380,000	18,190,000	**	n.a.	n.a.
74	7,229,573	170,916	4.2	170,916	4.2
75	7,089,068	n.a.	n.a.	n.a.	n.a.

[1] Direct giving and company foundation payouts included; grants made to and retained by company foundations are excluded.

[2] U.S. and worldwide pretax income rounded, percentages actual.

* Company showed loss.

** Less than 0.1 percent

n.a.=Not available.

Table 13: 75 Top Donors, Cash and Noncash Giving, 1990

Company Rank	Total Contributions (Dollars)	Cash	Cash as % of Total	Securities	Securities as % of Total	Company Product	Company Product as % of Total	Property & Equipment	Property & Equipment as % of Total
1	$101,400,000	$78,200,000	77%	$0	0%	$14,400,000	14%	$ 8,800,000	9%
2	65,300,000	43,100,000	66	0	0	0	0	22,200,000	34
3	51,813,374	35,938,946	69	0	0	15,874,428	31	0	0
4	46,637,106	45,700,955	98	0	0	0	0	936,151	2
5	45,400,000	45,400,000	100	0	0	0	0	0	0
6	37,913,600	37,913,600	100	0	0	0	0	0	0
7	37,200,000	22,100,000	59	0	0	15,100,000	41	0	0
8	36,914,100	36,599,220	99	0	0	203,925	1	110,955	*
9	32,120,700	26,687,700	83	0	0	5,258,000	16	175,000	1
10	31,100,143	15,921,442	51	0	0	15,178,701	49	0	0
11	30,731,854	30,731,854	100	0	0	0	0	0	0
12	30,667,792	9,726,715	32	0	0	20,941,077	68	0	0
13	29,200,000	27,569,438	94	0	0	682,781	2	947,781	3
14	28,789,763	9,798,999	34	0	0	18,990,764	66	0	0
15	26,417,984	26,349,179	99	0	0	0	0	68,805	*
16	26,335,000	24,221,000	92	0	0	0	0	2,114,000	8
17	24,544,913	14,098,803	57	0	0	10,263,360	42	182,750	1
18	23,381,475	23,381,475	100	0	0	0	0	0	0
19	22,498,084	13,664,164	61	0	0	2,351,990	10	6,481,930	29
20	22,354,156	19,550,832	87	0	0	2,716,174	12	87,150	*
21	21,926,694	18,376,694	84	0	0	3,550,000	16	0	0
22	21,880,143	21,880,143	100	0	0	0	0	0	0
23	21,419,115	20,661,252	96	0	0	0	0	757,863	4
24	21,187,870	21,187,870	100	0	0	0	0	0	0
25	21,073,085	21,073,085	100	0	0	0	0	0	0
26	20,801,634	19,264,511	93	0	0	0	0	1,537,123	7
27	20,735,302	20,735,302	100	0	0	0	0	0	0
28	20,658,411	20,538,411	99	0	0	120,000	1	0	0
29	20,030,099	20,030,099	100	0	0	0	0	0	0
30	19,816,454	6,790,250	34	0	0	12,800,000	65	226,204	1
31	19,585,000	19,585,000	100	0	0	0	0	0	0
32	18,910,640	18,910,640	100	0	0	0	0	0	0
33	18,101,699	17,501,699	97	0	0	0	0	600,000	3
34	17,507,606	17,407,606	99	0	0	0	0	100,000	1
35	17,145,000	17,145,000	100	0	0	0	0	0	0
36	16,951,743	12,951,743	76	0	0	400,000	2	0	0
37	16,553,936	16,553,936	100	0	0	0	0	0	0
38	16,193,781	16,193,781	100	0	0	0	0	0	0
39	15,962,208	15,962,208	100	0	0	0	0	0	0
40	15,836,352	5,449,352	34	0	0	10,387,000	66	0	0
41	15,714,000	15,714,000	100	0	0	0	0	0	0
42	15,700,000	15,700,000	100	0	0	0	0	0	0
43	15,647,500	10,581,500	68	0	0	5,066,000	32	0	0
44	15,400,000	15,400,000	100	0	0	0	0	0	0
45	15,290,621	15,290,621	100	0	0	0	0	0	0
46	15,174,891	15,174,891	100	0	0	0	0	0	0
47	14,615,915	9,336,536	64	0	0	5,279,379	36	0	0
48	13,400,232	13,189,829	98	0	0	0	0	0	0
49	13,342,800	13,342,800	100	0	0	0	0	210,403	*
50	13,015,517	13,015,517	100	0	0	0	0	0	0

Total in a row may not add to 100 due to rounding.

*Less than 1 percent.

Total row does not add up to 100% because company did not give details or breakdown of their cash and noncash contributions but only reported the total.

Table 13: 75 Top Donors, Cash and Noncash Giving, 1990 (continued)

Company Rank	Total Contributions (dollars)	Cash	Cash as % of Total	Securities	Securities as % of Total	Company Product	Company Product as % of Total	Property & Equipment	Property & Equipment as % of Total
51	$ 12,175,544	$12,175,544	100%	$ 0	0%	$ 0	0%	$ 0	0%
52	11,701,456	11,700,129	99	0	0	1,127	*	0	0
53	11,279,000	11,279,000	100	0	0	0	0	0	0
54	11,055,000	5,050,000	46	0	0	5,700,000	52	0	0
55	11,050,000	11,050,000	100	0	0	0	0	0	0
56	11,001,103	11,001,103	100	0	0	0	0	0	0
57	10,678,768	10,678,768	100	0	0	0	0	0	0
58	10,502,374	10,502,374	100	0	0	0	0	0	0
59	10,441,940	10,441,940	100	0	0	0	0	0	0
60	10,082,211	9,604,680	95	0	0	317,378	3	0	0
61	10,078,882	10,078,882	100	0	0	0	0	0	0
62	9,998,665	9,998,665	100	0	0	0	0	0	0
63	8,992,573	8,992,573	100	0	0	0	0	0	0
64	8,890,797	8,890,797	100	0	0	0	0	0	0
65	8,725,659	8,725,659	100	0	0	0	0	0	0
66	8,661,000	8,661,000	100	0	0	0	0	0	0
67	8,261,874	8,261,874	100	0	0	0	0	0	0
68	8,261,410	8,261,410	100	0	0	0	0	0	0
69	8,146,378	8,146,378	100	0	0	0	0	0	0
70	8,054,321	4,945,321	61	0	0	0	0	0	0
71	7,870,000	7,870,000	100	0	0	0	0	0	0
72	7,575,000	7,575,000	100	0	0	0	0	0	0
73	7,380,000	7,380,000	100	0	0	0	0	0	0
74	7,229,573	7,229,573	100	0	0	0	0	0	0
75	7,089,068	7,089,068	100	0	0	0	0	0	0

Total in a row may not add to 100 due to rounding.

*Less than 1 percent.

Total row does not add up to 100% because company did not give details or breakdown of their cash and noncash contributions but only reported the total.

Table 14: Beneficiaries of the 75 Top Donors, 1990

Company Rank	Total Contributions (Dollars)	Health and Human Services	Education	Culture and Arts	Civic and Community	Other
1	$101,400,000	31%	41%	15%	6%	8%
2	65,300,000	19	60	7	10	4
3	51,813,374	16	63	12	6	3
4	46,637,106	22	33	15	8	23
5	45,400,000	28	31	23	13	5
6	37,913,600	13	57	9	20	1
7	37,200,000	45	21	6	9	16
8	36,914,100	17	52	18	13	0
9	32,120,700	0	42	0	0	58
10	31,100,143	37	30	14	15	4
11	30,731,854	26	5	43	25	1
12	30,667,792	26	51	12	11	0
13	29,200,000	18	55	6	13	2
14	28,789,763	24	71	3	2	0
15	26,417,984	20	47	9	20	4
16	26,335,000	28	32	16	15	9
17	24,544,913	17	26	10	6	41
18	23,381,475	49	24	5	20	2
19	22,498,084	25	48	20	4	3
20	22,354,156	25	54	2	18	1
21	21,926,694	9	60	4	11	16
22	21,880,143	21	31	14	7	27
23	21,419,115	27	42	8	18	4
24	21,187,870	14	53	14	19	0
25	21,073,085	25	59	7	8	1
26	20,801,634	22	49	6	14	9
27	20,735,302	34	34	17	14	1
28	20,658,411	41	22	6	10	13
29	20,030,099	87	0	0	0	13
30	19,816,454	16	41	5	35	2
31	19,585,000	32	46	13	8	1
32	18,910,640	13	49	23	15	0
33	18,101,699	37	28	7	24	4
34	17,507,606	20	50	10	3	17
35	17,145,000	33	46	15	6	0
36	16,951,743	21	54	8	9	8
37	16,553,936	50	28	10	9	3
38	16,193,781	31	17	2	29	21
39	15,962,208	23	37	10	26	4
40	15,836,352	25	36	15	14	10
41	15,714,000	33	36	15	15	1
42	15,700,000	62	21	2	6	9
43	15,647,500	32	34	25	7	2
44	15,400,000	27	46	6	19	1
45	15,290,621	22	37	25	13	4
46	15,174,891	41	26	21	7	6
47	14,615,915	12	31	2	20	33
48	13,400,232	34	47	10	8	1
49	13,342,800	29	44	5	19	3
50	13,015,517	25	34	17	24	0

Total in a row may not add to 100 percent due to rounding.

Table 14: Beneficiaries of the 75 Top Donors, 1990 (continued)

Company Rank	Total Contributions (Dollars)	Health and Human Services	Education	Culture and Arts	Civic and Community	Other
51	$12,175,544	32%	37%	5%	25%	0%
52	11,701,456	28	46	13	11	3
53	11,279,000	22	15	0	0	63
54	11,055,000	70	22	4	4	0
55	11,050,000	30	16	14	0	1
56	11,001,103	21	50	17	11	1
57	10,678,768	27	19	21	17	16
58	10,502,374	32	28	26	14	0
59	10,441,940	21	20	9	15	2
60	10,082,211	44	20	9	19	1
61	10,078,882	4	58	17	21	0
62	9,998,665	37	42	8	13	0
63	8,992,573	27	48	16	8	1
64	8,890,797	29	51	12	7	1
65	8,725,659	35	46	7	9	3
66	8,661,000	24	33	23	12	8
67	8,261,874	8	65	11	16	6
68	8,261,410	17	31	16	25	11
69	8,146,378	33	34	12	15	6
70	8,054,321	28	6	3	39	24
71	7,870,000	0	100	0	0	0
72	7,575,000	5	20	49	15	11
73	7,380,000	42	27	4	27	0
74	7,229,573	53	22	13	11	0
75	7,089,068	0	100	0	0	0

Total in a row may not add to 100 percent due to rounding.

Table 15: Corporate Assistance Expenditures, Summarized, 1990

Description	Number of Companies	Sum ($ Thousands)	Median
Cash disbursements to 501(c) (3) organizations not reported as charitable contributions	34	$48,954	$275,940
Loan of company personnel	31	9,817	50,000
Donations of product and property not reported as charitable contributions	29	12,690	75,760
Use of corporate facilities or services	34	3,476	29,531
Loans at below-market yields	11	1,750	40,000
Administrative cost for contributions function	53	23,677	162,000
Total	192	$101,768	$332,997

Totals may not add due to rounding.

Table 16: Corporate Assistance Expenditures, by Industry, 1990

Industry Classification	Number of Companies	Sums		Medians	
		Total Corporate Assistance ($ Thousands)	Corporate Assistance as Percent of Total Contributions	Total Corporate Assistance	Corporate Assistance as Percent of Total Contributions
Chemicals	9	$ 6,337	4%	$ 274,000	11%
Computers/office equipment	4	3,467	2	1,037,500	18
Electrical machinery (not computer)	3	10,735	*	*	*
Food/beverage/tobacco	3	15,656	*	*	*
Machinery, nonelectrical	3	1,648	*	*	*
Paper and like products	2	543	*	*	*
Petroleum and gas[1]	9	25,915	12	1,500,000	10
Pharmaceuticals	5	3,545	2	424,668	5
Primary metals	3	1,905	*	*	*
Printing/publishing/media	1	190	*	*	*
Transportation equipment[2]	6	8,282	4	877,524	14
Other manufacturing[3]	3	874	*	*	*
Total: Manufacturing	51	$79,097	6%	$ 500,000	10%
Banking	12	7,930	7	220,952	24
Finance	1	860	*	*	*
Insurance	17	5,353	4	160,600	16
Retail and wholesale trade	1	370	*	*	*
Telecommunications	3	8,656	*	*	*
Transportation	3	457	*	*	*
Utilities	10	6,376	10	392,514	18
Other services[4]	1	230	*	*	*
Total: Nonmanufacturing	48	$30,232	6%	$228,241	16%
Total: All Companies	99	$109,329	6%	$297,561	13%

[1] Includes mining companies.

[2] Includes tire manufacturers.

[3] Includes fabricated metal products, and stone, clay and glass products.

[4] Includes engineering and construction companies.

* Totals include all cases, but details omit industries with fewer than 4 cases.

Table 17: 75 Top Social Expenditure Donors,

Corporate Social Expenditures as a Percent of Pretax Income, 1990

Company Rank	Total of Corporate Assistance and Contributions	Corporate Social Expenditure as a Percent of		Rank for Corporate Assistance Only	Rank for Cash Only
		U.S. Pretax Income	Worldwide Pretax Income		
1	$ 55,897,400	n.a.%	0.9%	3	2
2	50,920,755	2.5	0.6	1	5
3	39,150,000	6.2	2.4	13	14
4	30,563,400	1.6	0.7	21	9
5	29,764,763	7.2	2.8	31	56
6	28,759,510	2.1	0.8	10	11
7	27,835,000	1.6	1.4	18	12
8	27,758,578	1.5	1.5	4	18
9	24,387,115	1.3	0.6	9	19
10	24,385,000	n.a.	1.2	7	22
11	23,505,000	n.a.	1.7	2	41
12	20,780,208	n.a.	1.0	6	32
13	20,036,454	3.6	3.1	57	74
14	19,476,606	3.0	2.4	12	28
15	16,600,000	n.a.	n.a.	n.a.	36
16	16,059,837	n.a.	2.6	5	50
17	13,380,037	n.a.	1.3	15	46
18	12,508,541	n.a.	2.0	46	45
19	12,276,514	12.8	11.0	14	52
20	12,131,151	2.2	0.9	27	49
21	11,479,668	n.a.	1.1	43	94
22	10,454,641	n.a.	n.a.	n.a.	53
23	10,243,742	n.a.	2.5	17	62
24	10,198,665	n.a.	2.0	60	55
25	7,212,900	n.a.	0.9	20	81
26	6,875,151	3.6	3.6	n.a.	143
27	6,348,000	1.8	1.8	n.a.	95
28	6,129,044	2.2	1.9	33	90
29	5,734,800	n.a.	0.3	n.a.	92
30	5,472,321	3.5	1.7	29	109
31	5,448,621	n.a.	1.7	24	111
32	5,380,000	3.6	1.4	40	100
33	5,268,563	1.5	0.8	n.a.	117
34	5,225,331	n.a.	0.9	n.a.	124
35	5,191,850	n.a.	0.4	n.a.	128
36	5,100,701	6.0	4.3	42	102
37	4,846,954	3.4	3.4	n.a.	104
38	4,748,119	n.a.	n.a.	45	106
39	4,610,054	n.a.	0.7	74	105
40	4,265,000	1.5	0.1	49	230
41	3,992,074	1.0	1.0	38	133
42	3,838,000	n.a.	2.3	28	145
43	3,703,299	1.2	1.2	62	130
44	3,656,571	n.a.	1.7	39	138
45	3,558,000	n.a.	0.8	51	136
46	3,349,252	3.4	3.3	n.a.	137
47	3,316,510	1.0	1.0	32	158
48	3,231,247	n.a.	1.9	44	150
49	3,153,684	36.5	n.a.	37	157
50	2,994,612	0.5	0.5	22	200

n.a.=Not available.

Note: Companies in this table are only those that reported corporate assistance expenditures in addition to their charitable contributions.

Table 17: 75 Top Social Expenditure Donors (continued)

Company Rank	Total of Corporate Assistance and Contributions	Corporate Social Expenditure as a Percent of		Rank for Corporate Assistance Only	Rank for Cash Only
		U.S. Pretax Income	Worldwide Pretax Income		
51	$ 2,923,120	n.a.	0.8%	83	155
52	2,860,000	1.6%	1.6	11	252
53	2,705,015	0.6	0.6	48	166
54	2,705,000	n.a.	0.9	36	170
55	2,637,034	n.a.	0.7	63	159
56	2,613,075	n.a.	0.6	98	149
57	2,598,175	n.a.	0.6	94	151
58	2,520,000	0.3	0.3	n.a.	162
59	2,478,514	1.9	1.3	76	163
60	2,338,561	1.3	13.1	89	164
61	2,321,414	0.4	0.4	41	177
62	2,165,600	n.a.	1.3	56	173
63	2,016,322	n.a.	1.7	68	176
64	1,994,419	0.9	0.6	79	175
65	1,826,087	1.1	1.1	47	198
66	1,811,540	0.6	0.6	88	182
67	1,780,394	n.a.	n.a.	59	193
68	1,764,249	n.a.	n.a.	n.a.	231
69	1,715,028	0.4	0.4	66	220
70	1,708,156	2.5	2.5	n.a.	189
71	1,633,741	0.3	1.1	52	208
72	1,487,000	0.8	0.7	n.a.	202
73	1,372,760	n.a.	n.a.	72	217
74	1,368,351	1.1	n.a.	n.a.	228
75	1,347,000	0.8	0.8	n.a.	225

n.a.=Not available.
Note: Companies in this table are only those that reported corporate assistance expenditures in addition to their charitable contributions.

**Table 18: Program Administration Cost
As a Percent of Contributions Budget**

Medians by Size of Contributions Budget

Size of Contributions Budget	Number of Companies	Administrative Cost as a Percent of Contributions Budget (Median)
Less than $500,000	10	5.5%
$500,000 to $1 million	8	4.8
$1 million to $2.5 million	16	5.7
$2.5 million to $5 million	13	6.9
$5 million and over	18	4.2
Total	65	5.1%

Median Value of Administrative Costs: $162,000

Table 19: Number of Foundations

Companies Grouped by Industry Class

Industry Classification	Number of Companies	Number of Foundations	Percent of Companies With Foundations
Chemicals	21	12	57%
Computers/office equipment	9	3	33
Electrical machinery (not computer)	11	7	64
Food/beverage/tobacco............................	14	7	50
Machinery, nonelectrical	8	5	62
Paper and like products	11	6	54
Petroleum and gas[1]	22	5	23
Pharmaceuticals	13	7	54
Primary metals	11	5	45
Printing/publishing/media	7	3	43
Textiles and apparel	2	1	50
Transportation equipment[2]	17	5	29
Other manufacturing[3]	17	10	59
Total: Manufacturing	163	76	47%
Banking	42	16	38
Finance	6	2	33
Insurance...	35	12	34
Retail and wholesale trade	14	1	7
Telecommunications	13	4	31
Transportation	10	4	40
Utilities	36	10	28
Other services[4]	11	3	27
Total: Nonmanufacturing	167	52	31%
Total: All Companies	330	128	39%

[1] Includes mining companies.

[2] Includes tire manufacturers.

[3] Includes fabricated metal products, and stone, clay and glass products.

[4] Includes engineering and construction companies.

Table 20: Foundations, Relationship Between Payouts and Payins, 1986 to 1990

(millions of dollars)

Category	1990	1989	1988	1987	1986
Grants to company foundations	$414.6	$412.7	$433.6	$486.8	$649.1
Contributions by company foundations	889.2	751.5	702.9	609.9	641.0
Payouts less payins	470.1	338.9	269.3	123.1	(8.1)
Percent payouts exceeded payins	113.4%	82.1%	62.1%	25.3%	-1.3%

Table 21: Flow of Funds Into and Out of Foundations, 1986 to 1990

	1990		1989		1988		1987		1986	
	Number of Companies	Percent of Total	Number of Companies	Percent of Total	Number of Companies	Percent of Total	Number of Companies	Percent of Total	Number of Companies	Percent of Total
Payins equal to payouts	25	20%	29	13%	11	9%	26	12%	22	9%
Payins less than payouts	56	44	135	63	60	48	120	56	136	57
Payins greater than payouts	46	36	50	24	53	43	67	32	82	34
Total	127	100%	214	100%	124	100%	213	100%	240	100%

Table 22: Sources of Corporate Contributions, 1986 to 1990

(millions of dollars)

	1990		1989		1988		1987		1986	
Total company contributions	$1,560.2	(328)	$1,481.2	(318)	$1,376.4	(345)	$1,555.2	(315)	$1,688.6	(353)
Less: Grants to company foundations	414.6	(329)	412.7	(127)	433.6	(129)	486.8	(129)	649.1	(157)
Direct company contributions	1,145.6	(329)	1,068.6	(294)	942.8	(327)	1,068.5	(293)	1,039.5	(334)
Plus: Contributions by company foundations	889.2	(330)	751.5	(200)	702.9	(204)	609.9	(196)	641.0	(224)
Total corporate contributions	2,051.5	(330)	$1,820.1	(333)	$1,645.7	(356)	$1,678.3	(328)	$1,680.4	(372)

(Numbers in parentheses are responding companies.)

Table 23: Anticipated Changes in Contributions Budgets, 1990 to 1991

by Industry

Industry Classification	Number of Companies	1990-1991 Average Anticipated Percentage Change	1990-1991 Median Anticipated Percentage Change
Chemicals	19	- 4%	n.a.
Computers/office equipment	6	1	- 1
Electrical machinery (not computer)	9	* *	n.a.
Food/beverage/tobacco	11	1	2
Machinery, nonelectrical	7	13	4
Paper and like products	9	- 12	- 5
Petroleum and gas[1]	17	**	**
Pharmaceuticals	10	7	9
Primary metals	8	- 5	- 3
Printing/publishing/media	5	- 5	2
Textiles and apparel	*	23	23
Transportation equipment[2]	14	* *	* *
Other manufacturing[3]	15	* *	* *
Total: Manufacturing	132	* *	* *
Banking	30	4	1
Finance	5	* *	4
Insurance	30	3	2
Retail and wholesale trade	8	- 4	* *
Telecommunications	11	5	2
Transportation	8	- 1	2
Utilities	26	4	4
Other services[4]	9	15	12
Total: Nonmanufacturing	127	4%	3%
Total: All Companies	259	2%	2%

1 Includes mining companies.
2 Includes tire manufacturers.
3 Includes fabricated metal products, and stone, clay and glass products.
4 Includes engineering and construction companies.
* Fewer than 4 companies reported.
** Less than 1 percent.
n.a. = not available

Table 24: Anticipated Changes in Contributions Budgets, 1990 to 1991

By Program Size

Program Size	Number of Companies	Median Percentage Increase 1990-1991
Less than $500,000	33	4.4%
$500,000 to $1 million	36	4.5
$1 million to $2.5 million	56	1.5
$2.5 million to $5 million	51	- 0.4
$5 million and over	83	0.9
Total	259	1.6%

Table 25: Giving by Regional Headquarters, 1990

Region	Number of Companies	Total Contributions ($ Millions)	Health and Human Services			Education	Culture and Arts	Civic and Community	Other	Unspecified
			Federated Campaigns	Other Health and Human Services	Total Health and Human Services					
New England: .... (Maine, New Hampshire, Vermont, Massachusetts, Rhode Island, Connecticut)	32	$ 213.4	16%	8%	30%	38%	10%	12%	9%	1%
Middle Atlantic: .... (New York, New Jersey, Pennsylvania)	74	636.3	12	10	28	39	14	11	8	*
East North Central: .... (Illinois, Ohio, Indiana Michigan, Wisconsin)	79	510.1	11	10	25	41	10	14	6	4
West North Central: .... (Iowa, Kansas, Minnesota, Missouri, Nebraska, North Dakota, South Dakota)	34	192.3	12	12	30	30	18	14	5	4
South Atlantic: .... (Delaware, District of Columbia, Florida, Georgia, Maryland, North Carolina, South Carolina, Virginia, West Virginia, Puerto Rico, Virgin Islands)	36	135.6	13	10	28	40	14	12	6	1
East South Central: .... (Alabama, Kentucky, Mississippi, Tennessee)	9	15.5	9	12	24	45	12	9	10	*
West South Central: .... (Arkansas, Louisiana, Oklahoma, Texas)	24	130.6	17	2	26	42	8	13	6	5
Mountain: .... (Arizona, Colorado, Idaho, Montana, Nevada, New Mexico, Utah, Wyoming)	4	5.3	9	6	18	22	6	40	14	1
Pacific: .... (Alaska, California, Guam, Hawaii, Oregon, Washington)	38	212.3	16	12	34	38	9	11	9	*
Total	330	$2,051.4	13%	10%	28%	38%	12%	12%	7%	2%

*Less than 1 percent.
Total for a region may not add to 100 percent because of rounding.

Quartile Tables

Note: In each table using medians or quartiles, the data for each group (e.g., an industry class, an asset or income-size group) are placed in rank order from the lowest to the highest value, and divided into quarters. The first quartile is 25 percent of the way from the bottom number in the ranking; the median is the middle value in the ranking; and the third quartile is then 75 percent of the way between the lowest and the highest value. The "total" line on each table provides the quartiles (or median) for all of the companies included in that table.

Table 26: Contributions as a Percent of Worldwide Pretax Income—Quartiles, 1980 to 1990

	Lower Quartile	Median	Upper Quartile
1980	0.37%	0.66%	1.16%
1981	0.40	0.72	1.23
1982	0.53	0.99	1.62
1983	0.52	0.94	1.65
1984	0.53	0.85	1.54
1985	0.58	0.99	1.60
1986	0.59	1.01	1.63
1987	0.50	0.85	1.64
1988	0.51	0.83	1.30
1989	0.6	0.9	1.4
1990	0.6	1.0	1.9

Table 27A: Contributions as a Percent of U.S. Pretax Income—Quartiles, 1990

Companies Grouped by Dollar Size of Program

Program Size	Number of Companies	Lower Quartile	Median	Upper Quartile
Less than $500,000	27	0.5%	0.8%	1.1%
$500,000 to $1 million	19	0.5	1.0	1.9
$1 million to $2.5 million	48	0.4	0.8	1.4
$2.5 million to $5 million	29	1.1	1.5	3.3
$5 million and over	42	1.3	1.9	3.5
All Groups	165	0.6	1.2	2.1

Table 27B: Contributions as a Percent of Worldwide Pretax Income—Quartiles, 1990

Companies Grouped by Dollar Size of Program

Program Size	Number of Companies	Lower Quartile	Median	Upper Quartile
Less than $500,000	39	0.4%	0.6%	1.0%
$500,000 to $1 million	33	0.6	0.8	1.6
$1 million to $2.5 million	63	0.5	0.7	1.6
$2.5 million to $5 million	53	0.7	1.2	1.7
$5 million and over	86	0.9	1.3	2.2
All Groups	274	0.6	1.0	1.9

Table 28A: Contributions as a Percent of U.S. Pretax Income—Quartiles, 1990

Companies Grouped by Size of U.S. Income

| U.S. Pretax Income | Number of Companies | Contributions Ratios[1] | | |
		Lower Quartile	Median	Upper Quartile
$10 to 24.9 million	11	1.0%	1.9%	2.2%
$25 to 49.9 million	14	1.1	1.5	2.0
$50 to 99.9 million	22	0.7	1.4	3.3
$100 to 249.9 million	40	0.7	1.0	1.9
$250 to 499.9 million	28	0.6	1.1	1.5
$500 to 999.9 million	23	0.3	1.2	2.8
$1 billion and over	22	0.2	1.1	1.6
All Income Groups	**165**	**0.6**	**1.2**	**2.1**

[1] The statistics presented here are derived only from companies with positive income.

Table 28B: Contributions as a Percent of Worldwide Pretax Income—Quartiles, 1990

Companies Grouped by Size of Worldwide Income

| Worldwide Pretax Income | Number of Companies | Contributions Ratios[1] | | |
		Lower Quartile	Median	Upper Quartile
$10 to 24.9 million	15	0.8%	1.9%	4.3%
$25 to 49.9 million	20	0.9	1.7	2.5
$50 to 99.9 million	22	0.6	0.9	2.1
$100 to 249.9 million	72	0.6	0.9	1.9
$250 to 499.9 million	55	0.6	1.0	1.4
$500 to 999.9 million	36	0.6	0.8	2.0
$1 billion and over	49	0.6	0.9	1.1
All Income Groups	**274**	**0.6**	**1.0**	**1.9**

[1] The statistics presented here are derived only from companies with positive income.

Table 29A: Contributions as a Percent of U.S. Pretax Income—Quartiles, 1990

Companies Grouped by Industry Class

Industrial Classification	Number of Companies	Contributions Ratios[1]		
		Lower Quartile	Median	Upper Quartile
Chemicals	12	1.3%	1.7%	2.6%
Food/beverage/tobacco	7	1.0	1.1	2.8
Machinery, nonelectrical	4	1.0	1.2	1.5
Paper and like products	5	1.9	3.4	4.5
Petroleum and gas[2]	11	1.0	1.5	1.9
Pharmaceuticals	8	1.3	1.8	3.0
Primary metals	2	0.2	1.2	2.1
Transportation equipment[3]	6	2.0	3.1	5.1
Other manufacturing[4]	6	0.8	0.9	1.9
Banking	24	1.1	1.9	2.8
Finance	2	0.8	2.2	3.6
Insurance	20	0.3	0.8	1.8
Retail and wholesale trade	6	0.6	2.3	4.7
Telecommunications	10	0.6	0.9	1.1
Transportation	5	0.8	0.9	1.2
Utilities	31	0.3	0.5	0.7

[1] The statistics presented here are derived only from companies with positive income.

[2] Includes mining companies.

[3] Includes tire manufacturers.

[4] Includes fabricated metal products, and stone, clay and glass products.

Table 29B: Contributions as a Percent of Worldwide Pretax Income—Quartiles, 1990

Companies Grouped by Industry Class

Industrial Classification	Number of Companies	Contributions Ratios[1]		
		Lower Quartile	Median	Upper Quartile
Chemicals	20	0.7%	0.9%	1.4%
Computers/office equipment	7	1.0	1.6	4.3
Electrical machinery (not computer)	10	0.7	1.0	1.8
Food/beverage/tobacco	13	0.9	1.1	1.7
Machinery, nonelectrical	8	0.6	0.7	1.0
Paper and like products	10	0.8	1.4	3.2
Petroleum and gas[2]	21	0.5	0.8	1.3
Pharmaceuticals	12	0.7	1.1	1.8
Primary metals	8	0.3	0.8	1.7
Printing/publishing/media	6	0.7	1.2	2.3
Transportation equipment[3]	13	1.0	2.0	2.6
Other manufacturing[4]	17	0.7	0.9	1.9
Banking	32	0.8	1.5	2.3
Finance	4	0.7	0.8	1.5
Insurance	15	0.5	0.9	2.0
Retail and wholesale trade	13	0.7	2.1	3.5
Telecommunications	13	0.6	0.9	1.1
Transportation	10	0.8	1.2	1.8
Utilities	33	0.3	0.5	0.7
Other services[5]	7	0.7	1.0	2.0

[1] The statistics presented here are derived only from companies with positive income.

[2] Includes mining companies.

[3] Includes tire manufacturers.

[4] Includes fabricated metal products, and stone, clay and glass products.

[5] Includes engineering and construction companies

Table 30A: Contributions as a Percent of U.S. Pretax Income—Quartiles, 1990

Companies Grouped by Size of U.S. Assets

Assets	Number of Companies	Contributions Ratios[1]		
		Lower Quartile	Median	Upper Quartile
Less than $500 million	23	0.6%	0.8%	1.7%
$500 to 999 million	13	0.8	1.2	1.7
$1 to 1.9 billion	22	0.5	0.9	1.3
$2 to 2.9 billion	11	0.5	0.8	2.0
$3 to 3.9 billion	8	0.9	1.6	3.5
$4 to 4.9 billion	7	1.2	1.9	4.5
$5 to 9.9 billion	32	0.5	1.2	2.8
$10 billion and over	49	0.9	1.4	2.5
All Asset Groups	**165**	**0.6**	**1.2**	**2.1**

[1] The statistics presented here are derived only from companies with positive income.

Table 30B: Contributions as a Percent of Worldwide Pretax Income—Quartiles, 1990

Companies Grouped by Size of Worldwide Assets

Assets	Number of Companies	Contributions Ratios[1]		
		Lower Quartile	Median	Upper Quartile
Less than $500 million	18	0.6%	0.9%	1.6%
$500 to 999 million	22	0.6	1.1	1.8
$1 to 1.9 billion	43	0.5	0.8	1.6
$2 to 2.9 billion	23	0.7	1.0	1.7
$3 to 3.9 billion	18	0.7	0.9	1.7
$4 to 4.9 billion	11	0.8	1.9	2.8
$5 to 9.9 billion	54	0.6	1.0	2.1
$10 billion and over	85	0.6	0.9	1.8
All Asset Groups	**274**	**0.6**	**1.0**	**1.9**

[1] The statistics presented here are derived only from companies with positive income.

Table 31A: Contributions as a Percent of U.S. Pretax Income—Quartiles, 1990

Companies Grouped by Size of U.S. Sales

U.S. Sales	Number of Companies	Contributions Ratios[1]		
		Lower Quartile	Median	Upper Quartile
Less than $250 million	32	0.5%	1.5%	2.4%
$250 to $500 million	5	0.6	0.8	1.4
$500 million to $1 billion	27	0.5	0.8	1.7
$1 billion to $2.5 billion	34	0.7	1.2	1.9
$2.5 billion to $5 billion	26	0.3	0.8	1.2
$5 billion and over	41	1.1	1.6	2.8
Total	165	0.6	1.2	2.1

[1] The statistics presented here are derived only from companies with positive income.

Table 31B: Contributions as a Percent of Worldwide Pretax Income—Quartiles, 1990

Companies Grouped by Size of Worldwide Sales

Worldwide Sales	Number of Companies	Contributions Ratios[1]		
		Lower Quartile	Median	Upper Quartile
Less than $250 million	46	0.6%	1.1%	1.9%
$250 to $500 million	9	0.5	0.6	0.8
$500 million to $1 billion	30	0.4	0.8	1.4
$1 billion to $2.5 billion	52	0.6	0.8	1.6
$2.5 billion to $5 billion	38	0.7	0.9	1.6
$5 billion and over	99	0.7	1.1	2.1
Total	274	0.6	1.0	1.9

[1] The statistics presented here are derived only from companies with positive income.

Table 32A: Contributions as a Percent of U.S. Pretax Income, 1990

Grouped by Rate of Giving

Contributions as Percent of Pretax Income	All Companies	Manufacturing	Banking	Insurance	Utilities and Telecommunications	Other Services
			(Number of Companies)[1]			
0 to .24%	14	1	1	3	9	9
.25 to .49	16	1	1	4	9	10
.50 to .74	20	4	n.a.	2	11	14
.75 to .99	18	5	3	4	3	6
1.0 to 1.49	34	21	4	1	7	8
1.5 to 1.99	19	11	6	2	n.a.	n.a.
2.0 to 2.99	19	11	4	1	n.a.	3
3.0 to 3.99	7	4	2	n.a.	n.a.	1
4.0 to 4.99	6	2	1	1	1	2
5.0 and over	12	6	2	2	1	2
Total	165	66	24	20	41	55

[1] Loss companies excluded.
n.a. = not available

Table 32B: Contributions as a Percent of Worldwide Pretax Income, 1990

Grouped by Rate of Giving

Contributions as Percent of Pretax Income	All Companies	Manufacturing	Banking	Insurance	Utilities and Telecommunications	Other Services
			(Number of Companies)[1]			
0 to .24%	15	6	2	1	6	6
.25 to .49	27	12	1	1	11	13
.50 to .74	60	34	3	3	12	20
.75 to .99	43	23	5	3	7	12
1.0 to 1.49	42	24	5	2	8	11
1.5 to 1.99	27	14	6	2	n.a.	5
2.0 to 2.99	30	18	5	1	n.a.	6
3.0 to 3.99	12	8	1	n.a.	n.a.	3
4.0 to 4.99	7	1	2	1	1	3
5.0 and over	11	7	2	1	1	1
Total	274	147	32	15	46	80

[1] Loss companies excluded.
n.a. = not available

Table 33: Beneficiaries of Company Support—Quartiles, 1990

Companies Grouped by Dollar Size of Program

Program Size	Number of Companies	Health and Human Services			Education			Culture and Arts		
		Lower Quartile	Median	Upper Quartile	Lower Quartile	Median	Upper Quartile	Lower Quartile	Median	Upper Quartile
Less than $500,000	48	32.4%	43.9%	56.0%	16.2%	20.3	40.3%	3.3%	9.0%	13.2%
$500,000 to $1 million	45	25.8	43.9	53.0	18.2	25.6	36.3	5.8	9.3	12.8
$1 million to $2.5 million	76	26.1	38.8	51.6	24.4	31.8	39.9	5.1	9.4	14.0
$2.5 million to $5 million	62	26.0	38.0	43.9	21.2	28.3	37.9	7.4	11.9	15.2
$5 million and over	99	18.2	16.2	45.4	26.8	36.0	48.9	5.8	10.4	15.5
All Groups	330	22.0	33.0	44.5	20.4	30.6	43.9	5.4	10.2	14.6

Program Size	Number of Companies	Civic and Community			Other		
		Lower Quartile	Median	Upper Quartile	Lower Quartile	Median	Upper Quartile
Less than $500,000	48	5.2%	11.1%	18.4%	0.2%	3.5%	9.6%
$500,000 to $1 million	45	4.8	9.9	19.9	0.1	1.6	3.1
$1 million to $2.5 million	76	4.5	9.6	15.6	0.3	0.7	1.2
$2.5 million to $5 million	62	7.0	11.3	18.2	0.2	0.8	2.8
$5 million and over	99	7.3	12.8	18.8	0.7	1.9	6.0
All Groups	330	6.0	10.8	17.9	0.4	1.3	3.7

Table 34: Beneficiaries of Company Support, 1990—Quartiles

Companies Grouped by Industry Class

Industry Category	Number of Companies	Health and Human Services			Education		
		Lower Quartile	Median	Upper Quartile	Lower Quartile	Median	Upper Quartile
Chemicals	21	20.0%	28.4%	34.6%	33.2%	42.8%	50.6%
Computers/office equipment	9	6.8	24.0	27.3	40.5	50.8	63.4
Electrical machinery (not computer)	11	*	21.7	28.9	24.0	36.3	51.3
Food/beverage/tobacco	14	26.7	30.2	37.8	17.9	25.5	30.8
Machinery, nonelectrical	8	41.3	44.4	49.4	24.5	29.3	35.6
Paper and like products	11	19.0	24.9	36.5	27.7	32.7	56.8
Petroleum and gas[1]	22	19.7	26.1	35.9	33.9	44.8	49.6
Pharmaceuticals	13	11.7	19.4	45.1	20.6	27.7	41.0
Primary metals	11	27.0	34.8	44.9	17.8	31.3	45.5
Printing/publishing/media	7	18.3	32.5	45.4	14.6	32.7	48.9
Transportation equipment[2]	17	20.6	26.7	35.0	42.1	46.6	53.6
Other manufacturing[3]	17	17.6	31.1	41.4	27.3	28.7	35.4
Total: Manufacturing	163	19.3	28.4	39.6	27.3	35.4	47.1
Banking	42	28.9	38.6	45.3	18.0	20.2	27.4
Finance	6	21.2	38.9	46.2	25.2	28.5	31.7
Insurance	35	32.9	41.4	50.9	23.7	31.6	36.6
Retail and wholesale trade	14	27.5	43.9	52.8	11.1	14.8	22.1
Telecommunications	13	19.6	30.4	33.1	33.3	35.8	48.2
Transportation	10	32.2	39.3	41.6	15.8	23.0	34.0
Utilities	36	31.3	43.4	53.9	18.5	20.6	29.4
Other services[4]	11	11.0	33.3	49.9	21.7	38.1	57.8
Total: Nonmanufacturing	167	29.6	39.5	49.8	18.5	25.0	34.2
Total: All Companies	330	22.0	33.0	44.5	20.4	30.6	43.9

[1] Includes mining companies.
[2] Includes tire manufacturers.
[3] Includes fabricated metal products, and stone, clay and glass products.
[4] Includes engineering and construction companies.
*Less than 0.1 percent.

Table 34: Beneficiaries of Company Support, 1990 —Quartile (continued)

Culture and Arts			Civic and Community			Other		
Lower Quartile	Median	Upper Quartile	Lower Quartile	Median	Upper Quartile	Lower Quartile	Median	Upper Quartile
6.0%	10.4%	15.0%	8.0%	12.4	16.2%	*%	2.0%	2.8%
1.7	2.6	11.8	1.6	6.0	18.2	0.4	1.3	7.8
—	4.9	12.4	—	4.8	12.0	1.2	22.6	28.4
5.1	11.0	21.3	7.1	12.5	15.2	1.0	2.8	6.6
7.9	9.8	13.4	5.9	8.0	15.2	0.2	0.6	3.9
4.4	10.9	14.2	8.3	14.2	19.6	0.1	0.2	2.8
7.1	9.4	13.6	6.0	11.3	18.4	0.7	1.8	4.6
2.2	5.1	9.5	5.6	9.1	19.3	1.1	3.1	33.5
3.8	7.1	12.2	3.3	7.9	13.4	0.1	1.4	2.9
9.5	12.6	23.2	2.4	8.4	17.3	0.2	0.2	2.4
7.4	9.6	13.9	8.2	9.4	11.4	0.7	1.0	1.9
3.8	9.0	12.0	7.5	12.1	24.6	0.6	0.8	9.4
4.5	9.2	13.6	4.8	10.2	16.2	0.4	1.3	3.9
9.5	13.9	15.9	6.8	14.4	23.5	1.9	3.5	4.7
11.3	16.6	21.4	7.3	9.8	10.8	3.3	3.3	3.3
5.4	10.6	13.9	5.0	8.1	19.4	0.1	0.2	0.8
2.7	5.4	9.3	2.7	15.2	23.6	2.6	9.0	20.5
11.8	15.4	17.0	6.0	7.4	14.4	0.8	1.6	3.1
1.9	10.8	16.7	6.1	10.1	23.9	0.9	0.9	0.9
8.4	10.2	13.5	9.2	14.7	23.1	0.6	1.0	2.2
—	13.8	15.6	5.3	11.0	13.5	14.5	14.5	14.5
5.9	11.1	15.4	6.3	11.6	19.8	0.3	1.4	3.5
5.4	10.2	14.6	6.0	10.8	17.9	0.4	1.3	3.7

Method Tables

Table 35: Participants by Size of Contributions Program, 1987 to 1990

Program Size	1990 Number	1990 Percent	1989 Number	1989 Percent	1988 Number	1988 Percent	1987 Number	1987 Percent
Less than $500,000	48	14%	79	24%	98	28%	74	23%
$500,000 to $1 million	45	14	44	13	69	19	62	19
$1 million to $2.5 million	76	23	68	20	108	30	111	34
$2.5 million to $5 million	62	19	55	17				
$5 million and over	99	30	87	26	81	23	81	25
Total	330		333		356		328	

Percentages may not add to 100 percent due to rounding.

Table 36A: Participants by U.S. Sales, 1990

U.S. Sales	Manufacturing Companies Number	Manufacturing Companies Percent	Selected Nonmanufacturing Companies [1] Number	Selected Nonmanufacturing Companies [1] Percent
Less than $250 million	70	43%	88	53%
$250 million to 500 million	2	1	5	3
$500 million to 1 billion	14	9	16	10
$1 billion to 2.5 billion	26	16	16	10
$2.5 billion to 5 billion	13	8	20	12
$5 billion and over	38	23	22	13
Total	163		167	

[1] Banking, insurance, telecommunications and utilities are excluded from nonmanufacturing companies and reported in Table 37A.
Percentages may not add to 100 due to rounding.

Table 36B: Participants by Worldwide Sales, 1990

Worldwide Sales	Manufacturing Companies		Selected Nonmanufacturing Companies [1]	
	Number	Percent	Number	Percent
Less than $250 million	22	14%	67	40%
$250 million to 500 million	4	2	5	3
$500 million to 1 billion	14	9	16	10
$1 billion to 2.5 billion	35	21	21	13
$2.5 billion to 5 billion	21	13	20	12
$5 billion and over	67	41	38	23
Total	163		167	

[1] Banking, insurance, telecommunications and utilities are excluded from nonmanufacturing companies and reported in Table 37B.
Percentages may not add to 100 due to rounding.

Table 37A: Participants by U.S. Assets, 1990: Banking, Insurance, Telecommunications, Gas and Electric Utilities

U.S. Assets	Banking		Insurance		Telecommunications		Utilities	
	Number	Percent	Number	Percent	Number	Percent	Number	Percent
Less than $250 million	10	24%	13	37%	3	23%	3	8%
$500 million to $1 billion	—	—	1	3	—	—	4	11
$1 billion to $2.5 billion	2	5	3	9	1	8%	6	17
$2.5 billion to $5 billion	3	7	4	11	3	23	5	14
$5 billion to $10 billion	6	14	4	11	—	—	11	31
$10 billion and over	21	50	10	29	6	46	7	19
Total	42		35		13		36	

Table 37B: Participants by Worldwide Assets, 1990: Banking, Insurance, Telecommunications, Gas and Electric Utilities, 1990

Worldwide Assets	Banking		Insurance		Telecommunications		Utilities	
	Number	Percent	Number	Percent	Number	Percent	Number	Percent
Less than $250 million	4	10%	18	51%	—	—%	—	—%
$500 million-$1 billion	1	2	3	9	—	—	4	11
$1 billion-$2.5 billion	3	7	—	—	1	8	7	19
$2.5 billion-$5 billion	4	10	2	6	2	15	5	14
$5 billion-$10 billion	6	14	3	9	1	8	11	31
$10 billion and over	24	57	9	25	9	69	9	25
Total	42		35		13		36	

Table 38: Manufacturing Participants in the Fortune 500

Based on Total Worldwide Sales

Rank		Number of Survey Respondents
Number	1- 100	66
	101- 200	27
	201- 300	26
	301- 400	10
	401- 500	9
	Total	138

Table 39: Nonmanufacturing Participants in the

Fortune Service 500

Industry Class (Top 500)	Number of Survey Respondents
Top 100 diversified service companies (ranked by sales)	17
Top 100 commercial banking companies (ranked by assets)	33
Top 50 savings institutions (ranked by assets)	3
Top 50 life insurance companies (ranked by assets)	18
Top 50 diversified financial companies (ranked by assets)	8
Top 50 retailing companies (ranked by sales)	9
Top 50 transportation companies (ranked by operating revenues)	5
Top 50 utilities (ranked by assets)	22
Total	115